DRIVING IT HOME

100 years of car advertising

PUBLISHED BY MIDDLESEX UNIVERSITY PRESS

SERIES INTRODUCTION

The twentieth century saw the advertising industry become a dominant driving force in Western culture. It was the engine of capitalism, directed political destinies and even influenced international conflict and military victories by means of propaganda. Advertising has become a defining element in our lives and culture, holding a mirror to our social history, values and aspirations.

'The historians and archaeologists will one day discover that the advertisements of our time are the richest and most faithful daily reflections that any society ever made of its entire range of activities.' (McLuhan, 1964, p.247)

This book is one of a series which describes the history of twentieth-century printed advertising. Each publication focuses on a different product. Most illustrations for this series come from The Library of Historic Advertising (LHA), an extensive collection of twentieth-century printed advertisements owned by Middlesex University and housed in the archives at their Cat Hill campus, London.

CONTENTS

Introduction

The story of the motor car (or 'automobile' as it's known in America) over the twentieth century has been the transformation of a practical, mechanical utility vehicle into a cultural icon, the epitome of modernity and a work of art. Filippo Tommaso Marinetti, the Italian founder of the Futurist movement, claimed that the contemporary automobile was more beautiful than ancient Greek sculpture: 'the magnificence of the world has been enriched by a new beauty, the beauty of speed' (Wollen and Kerr, 2002, p.22). This new modern icon symbolised the industrial and technological successes of the era and reflected society's hopes, fears and aspirations. As the years went by, the appearance of the motor car and the way in which it was represented in advertising often mirrored economic, political, military and social changes, presenting the history of the twentieth century in chrome, steel, and glass. As Quentin Willson remarks, 'Cars are the ultimate gods of an age that has always worshipped the machine' (Willson, 2001, p.8).

Car advertising in the twentieth century, perhaps more than the advertising for any other product, tells the story of the economic, political and social history of those years. The decision to buy a new car has always been a major financial commitment and is not one to be made on impulse or without full consideration, so advertising techniques for these products have had to be particularly persuasive. Huge amounts of money are spent on car advertising. Six billion euros was spent in Europe in 2000,

It's here!... It's new!... designed for you!...

the '51 DeSoto

THE RIDE IS A
Revelation

ILLUSTRATION i

1951

ILLUSTRATION ii

1949

THE MIGHTY CHRYSLER SARATOGA 2-DOOR HARDTOP, SPORTSWEAR BY SAKS FIFTH AVE.

The Man who owns it owns <u>more</u>!

EVERYWHERE TODAY...THOUSANDS OF MOTORISTS ARE DISCOVERING THAT IN THE THINGS THEY MOST WANT IN A CAR—LUXURY, COMFORT AND PERFORMANCE—THE MIGHTY CHRYSLER GIVES THEM MORE!

Today, there's no question about it—the man who owns the Mighty Chrysler owns *more* of the good things in motoring.

And *you* could, too.

You, too, could enjoy the reward of Chrysler ownership . . . the deep, personal pleasure of being far out front in styling and design.

You, too, could experience the greatest comforts and luxuries any car can offer—and all at no extra cost! The restfulness of Torsion-Aire Ride . . . the modern ease of Pushbutton TorqueFlite driving . . . the effortlessness of full-time Power Steering

. . . the safety of Total-Contact Brakes . . . the security of four-beam dual headlighting. Never before has any car been so beautifully engineered for the joy of driving!

What's more, you, too, could find satisfaction in all the "extra bonuses" this Mighty Chrysler gives you. Its outstanding fuel economy was established in the Mobilgas Economy Run.

Discover all this tomorrow at your Chrysler dealer's. See the all-new Chrysler Windsor, now in a lower-priced field . . . the fabulous new Chrysler Saratoga . . . and the glamorous new Chrysler New Yorker!

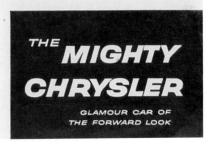

THE **MIGHTY** CHRYSLER

GLAMOUR CAR OF THE FORWARD LOOK

ILLUSTRATION iii

c. 1958

Corolla. For overprotective parents.

Dual airbags, self-tensioning seat belts, collapsible steering column, energy-absorbing reinforcements in the roof-side rails and pillars, side impact protection beams, rigid passenger safety cell, ABS and shatter-resistant glass. ⊕ TOYOTA

ILLUSTRATION iv

2000

and in the United States 10 billion dollars was spent in 2003. There is no doubt that this investment in advertising was worthwhile and that car advertising has been phenomenally successful; since 1970, the American car population has grown six times more quickly than the human population and double the rate of new drivers (Willson, 2001, p.9). However, times are changing: there is a growing realisation that our global dependency on the car is putting the future of our planet in jeopardy, that oil is running out and the fear of gridlock in our major cities is becoming a terrible reality. Many of the leading car companies are struggling and some have given up the fight. Essentially, as a machine, the motor car has changed little over the century, but now the future is in zero-emission vehicles, battery chargers and bio-fuels. Car advertising tells the story of a major element of twentieth-century industry, culture and life.

ILLUSTRATION v
Fortune, 1958

Chapter 1

1900–1920

From cycles to
Model Ts

At the beginning of the twentieth century the motor car was changing from a curious invention played with by the wealthy and adventurous, to a utilitarian and aesthetic passenger vehicle. The designs of cars at this time were still reminiscent of horse-drawn carriages: large wheels at the front, even larger wheels at the rear and the passengers sitting up high, unprotected from the elements. At this time, no one really knew what a car should look like – should it look like a horse-drawn carriage, a boat, a locomotive? In these early years, cars were produced by carriage manufacturers and often looked like a horse could be attached to the front if the engine failed.

Automobiles were certainly luxury items at this time. Many were designed to be chauffeur-driven and in America, in 1905, the price of cars ranged from $600 to $7,500 when the annual average income was only $450 (Gartman, 1994, p.33). In Britain, the average annual income was around £80 and the cost of cars ranged from about £200 to £800. Advertising in these early days did not always directly appeal to the social status of the privileged few who could afford to buy a car, nor did it attempt to appeal to those who may have been attracted by the thrill and pleasure associated with the speed of automobiles. This is in stark contrast to advertising for bicycles. During the Golden Age of bicycles, in the 1890s, these fashionable vehicles were presented in contemporary advertising as liberating, glamorous and

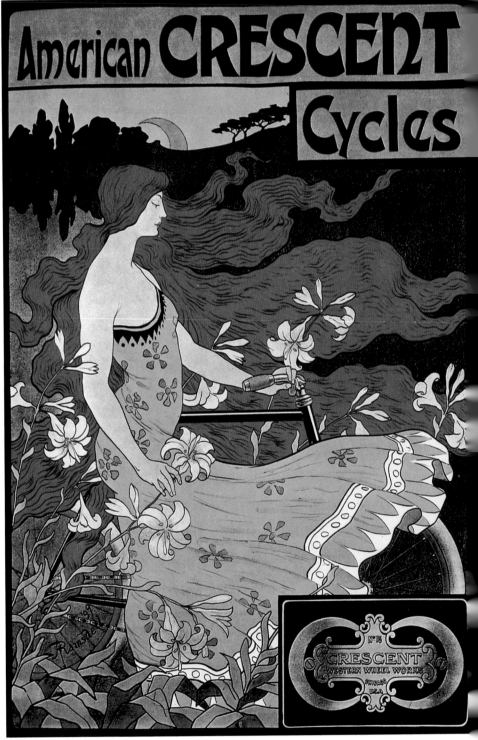

American **CRESCENT** Cycles

CRESCENT
WESTERN WHEEL WORKS

ILLUSTRATION 2

Punch, 1906

exhilarating. Images were daring and sensual, often portraying beautiful women liberated by the freedom cycling gave them ILLUSTRATION 1.

Perhaps reflecting the cautiousness with which people regarded the new, complex and unpredictable machinery of the automobile, advertising tended to be sober and reassuring, emphasising technical merits and reliability. A Daimler advertisement from 1906 ILLUSTRATION 2 is a rather dull affair, using its royal appointments to appeal to customers with social aspirations and citing such company virtues as 'experience' and 'organisation'. It seems that car manufacturers did not attract potential customers by extolling the thrills, speed and freedom of

ILLUSTRATION 3

The Graphic, 1909

Wolseley-Siddeley Autocars

By Appointment
to
H.M. the Queen.

"Perfect in Every Part!"

Absolute accuracy of construction from the most perfect materials, is the policy which has given the Wolseley-Siddeley Cars their leading position. For Reliability, Silence, and Low Running Costs they stand unrivalled, either for town use or country touring.

Descriptive Catalogue No. 36, showing Eight New Models,

posted on request.

e Wolseley Tool & Motor Car Co., Ltd.,

Proprietors: VICKERS, SONS & MAXIM, LTD.,

DERLEY PARK, BIRMINGHAM.

Telegrams: "Exactitude, Birmingham."   Telephone: Central 6153.

DON: York Street, Westminster.   MANCHESTER: 76, Deansgate.

The Wolseley-Siddeley Limousine Landaulette.

F 20.

driving, but with solid assurances that they would not be stuck in the middle of nowhere, in the rain, with a broken-down car. Again, a Wolseley-Siddeley advertisement from 1909 refers to 'accuracy of construction' ILLUSTRATION 3 hoping to appeal to nervous purchasers wary of the reputation of cars at that time as being uncomfortable and unreliable. Typical car advertisements of the day had a technical approach, displaying a simple side-on illustration or photograph of the car with columns of fine print listing mechanical features. Advertising tended to concentrate on the advantages of cars over horses. For example, the advantage that a car consumes fuel only when it is working!

HUMBER CYCLES and MOTORS

HAVE A WORLD-WIDE REPUTATION FOR SOUND BRITISH WORKMANSHIP.

CYCLES	COMPLETELY EQUIPPED. FULLY GUARANTEED.	FROM	**£10 10 0**
MOTOR CYCLES	CHAIN DRIVEN.	FROM	**£42 0 0**

immediate Delivery.   Easy Payments Arranged.

MOTOR CARS	4-CYLINDER.	12 H.P.	550 GNS.
		20 H.P.	750 GNS.

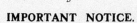

IMPORTANT NOTICE.

We are producing a two-seated light Car, which we shall shortly be prepared to supply at about 120 Guineas.

ART CATALOGUE SENT ON APPLICATION.

No. 85

HUMBER, LIMITED,

CYCLE MANUFACTURERS BY ROYAL WARRANTS TO H.M. KING EDWARD VII. & H.R.H. THE PRINCE OF WALES.

LONDON DEPOT: 32, HOLBORN VIADUCT, E.C.   WORKS: BEESTON (NOTTS) & COVENTRY.

ILLUSTRATION 4

The Graphic, 1903

Many car manufacturers at the beginning of the century started off in the bicycle industry. The bicycle boom financed vehicular inventions and engineering design which fuelled the development of the automobile. Trade marks such as Peugeot, Sunbeam, Opel, Rover and Triumph, began as names for cycle brands. An advertisement for Humber Cycles and Motors dated 1903 ILLUSTRATION 4 shows how companies started to move to motor vehicle production as the demand for cycles declined. Of course, the automobile industry would not have been so successful so soon, if the demands of the bicycle craze had not ensured some improvements in road conditions, particularly in America where the Office of Public Roads was established in 1893 to promote rural road development. Additionally, the car industry benefited from the development of the pneumatic tyre which had essentially been financed by the bicycle industry.

John Boyd Dunlop, a Scottish vet who lived in Belfast, is often credited with the invention of the pneumatic tyre. He created inflated canvas tubes with a rubber exterior which were designed to reduce the bumps and vibrations experienced by his young son on his bicycle. He patented his invention in 1889 and the Dunlop company was founded in that year. Dunlop's patent was later challenged by another Scot, Robert William Thomson, who had patented a similar design in 1846, but at that time, rubber had been extremely expensive and the idea was not exploited. Dunlop's idea had coincided with bicycle fever, and so his invention was timely. The first public appearance of pneumatic tyres on a motor vehicle was in 1895 when Andrè Michelin drove his Peugeot in a race from Paris to Bordeaux. Most cars at that time had solid rubber or iron wheels and Michelin's pneumatic ones were not initially very successful, being prone to numerous punctures on the rough roads.

At the beginning of the century, petrol cars were not the only cars one could buy. Steam cars and electric cars were also popular. In 1900, out of 8,000 automobiles owned in America, 5,000 were steam cars. An advertisement for Detroit Electric from 1916 ILLUSTRATION 5 illustrates the popularity in the United States of electric cars. Electric cars were virtually silent, easy to operate and popular with upper-class women. They were therefore often fitted with handcrafted coachwork befitting the wealthy customers to whom they appealed. The main problem linked with these

ILLUSTRATION 5

Saturday Evening Post, 1916

ILLUSTRATION 6

Collier's Weekly, 1912

electric cars was their short range on one battery charge and the fact that because they became particularly popular with women, they became associated with femininity and were therefore less attractive to male consumers. The Detroit Electric advertisement refers to the female members of the owner's family 'driving through the parks or on shopping errands', and emphasises the safety and simplicity of this kind of car. Steam cars were also being developed, especially as they eliminated the need for a gearbox. However, there were two major problems with steam cars – the length of time it took to raise steam from a cold start and the complexity of the engine. The petrol-powered car achieved predominance in the automobile market because of its relative ease of maintenance and the discovery of oil fields in Texas in 1901 which led to the reduction in oil prices and the wider availability of petrol.

Mass production changed the face of the automobile industry and made cars more affordable and available. The Oldsmobile Curved Dash Runabout was the first mass-produced car. Ransom Eli Olds was a pioneer of the American car industry. He founded the Olds Motor Vehicle Company in Lansing, Michigan in 1897. In the year 1901 Olds produced 425 cars from the first automotive assembly line at his Lansing factory. The following year the factory produced 2,500 cars. However, it was Henry Ford who used mass-production of automobiles to best advantage. He created the Ford Motor Company in 1903 in a converted wagon shop in Detroit. Ten years later the company was making half the cars in America. Ford had noticed that the market for high-priced automobiles for the very wealthy was becoming saturated and he believed that the future lay in making affordable motor cars for the masses. In 1908 he launched the Model T which sold for the reasonable price of $825, was relatively easy to drive and was sturdily built from high-quality steel in order to withstand the punishment of the rough roads.

The price was to fall every year until Ford ceased production of the Model T in 1927, by which time fifteen million units had been built and sold. An advertisement for the Model T **ILLUSTRATION 6** shows that by 1912 the price had fallen to $690 and the 'Torpedo' and 'Commercial Roadster' models sold for only $590. As is typical of car advertisements of the day, the emphasis is certainly on the technical aspects of the car with lengthy text, but atypically, Ford liked to emphasise the price. Other car manufacturers could not compete with Ford's prices and so rarely mentioned the prices in their advertising.

By 1915, in Europe, with war production paramount, the production of cars for civilian consumption had effectively ceased. Automobile factories started producing vehicles and aircraft to aid the war effort. In 1914, Daimler, Britain's oldest marque, produced engines for the first tanks ever built (known as 'Little Willie' and 'Big Willie'), as well as aeroplane engines and ambulances. An interesting

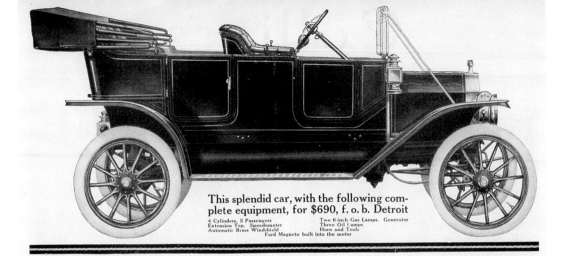

This splendid car, with the following complete equipment, for $690, f. o. b. Detroit

4 Cylinders, 5 Passengers   Two 6-inch Gas Lamps. Generator
Extension Top. Speedometer   Three Oil lamps
Automatic Brass Windshield   Horn and Tools
                 Ford Magneto built into the motor

Here's a Ford Model T Touring Car

$690

Handsome—Foredoors—roomy—up-to-the-minute in desired details, strong, simple and backed with a record of five years' satisfaction—giving results in all parts of the world to more than 100,000 users. This beautiful motor car completely equipped for only $690 f. o. b. Detroit.

FACTS from FORD

¶ There are no "glittering generalities" in FORD advertising.—It gives you the established Facts—we appeal to your judgment through Facts, not with claims—and you know it's more profitable to live with a Fact than to nurse a family of "claims."

¶ There's this about FORD advertising that makes it particularly distinctive and that is its positive harmony with Facts. It is just like FORD Model T—reliable, positive.

¶ We tell you FORD Model T is the lowest priced quality car and immediately follow with the Facts.

¶ Entire mechanical construction of Vanadium Steel, scientifically heat-treated—the very best as well as the most expensive steel made.

¶ The only motor car with the magneto built into the flywheel as a part of the motor; the only motor car in which there are neither dry cells nor batteries. This is also a FORD Magneto—built entirely in our own shops.

¶ The lightest weight 4-Cylinder motor car in the world, size, power and capacity considered—60 pounds to the horsepower.

¶ The cheapest 4-Cylinder motor car in maintenance, 20 to 25 miles on one gallon of gasoline and 5,000 to 8,000 miles on one set of tires.

¶ The simplest motor car in design, anybody of ordinary intelligence quickly understands its every mechanical detail.

¶ That it is a durable car is best evidenced by there being in active operation today more than 100,000 FORD cars; the most widely-known motor car, as it is seen in every part of the civilized world, it is the Universal Car.

¶ The FORD Model T has the lowest purchase price and running cost per mile per passenger of any motor car in the world.

¶ The high quality and low price of FORD Model T are possible because of:

¶ 1st: The extreme simplicity and accurately scientific design—the creation of the marvelous inventive genius of Henry Ford.

FACTS from FORD

¶ 2nd: The scientifically heat-treated Vanadium Steel material. We emphasize this because it is vitally important that you should know the sort of materials used in the construction of the motor car you buy.

¶ 3rd: The most efficient automobile factory in the world, where the workmen are employed during the entire year building only this ONE WONDERFUL CAR.

¶ 4th: The large production—75,000 FORD Model T cars in one year.

¶ 5th: The Ford Motor Company devotes all its energy to the production of only one car; it finances the entire business itself, and this is a mighty force in manufacture; no borrowed money, no interest-bearing bond issues, no mortgages, but everything bought and paid for with spot cash, and sold the same way.

¶ There is intense significance in the fact that every fifth car sold in America last year was a FORD Model T. This significance increases when you know that every third car made in America this year will be a FORD Model T.

¶ FORD Model T cars would not be made in such quantities if established merit had not produced the demand.

¶ FORD Model T car is in largest demand because of its all-round utility; it meets the motor car want of everybody, from the man of leisure to the busy worker, from the doctor and professional man to the banker and farmer.

¶ Remember all FORD cars are sold fully equipped—we specify the equipment article by article. When you buy a FORD Model T you buy a complete car.

¶ In addition to FORD Model T Touring Car we have for immediate delivery:

Ford Model T Torpedo, fully equipped, f. o. b. Detroit $590
Ford Model T Commercial Roadster, fully equipped, f. o. b. Detroit $590
Ford Model T Town Car, fully equipped, f. o. b. Detroit $900
Ford Model T Delivery Car, fully equipped, f. o. b. Detroit $700

¶ We have a new booklet just out, "Talks by the Jolly Fat Chauffeur with the Double Chin." Write for it. It is great. Branches and Large Distributors in all Large Cities. No Ford Cars Sold Unequipped.

Ford Motor Company

Detroit, Mich., U. S. A.

ILLUSTRATION 7

The Sphere, 1916

ILLUSTRATION 8

Motor, 1916

advertisement for Clincher Motor Tyres in 1916 ILLUSTRATION 7 appeals to the patriotic to buy British tyres rather than imported American tyres. In 1917, American car makers stopped production of private automobiles to make aeroplane engines and military vehicles for the war. They also initiated non-driving days in some parts of the country in order to conserve fuel. The First World War was also the first mechanised war

and thousands of men and women were taught how to drive and repair automobiles.

A British advertisement for the American Willys-Overland from 1916 shows a woman driving a car full of wounded soldiers ILLUSTRATION 8. A 1918 advertisement, again for Willys-Overland, gives an unusual over-head view of a woman driver with her passengers

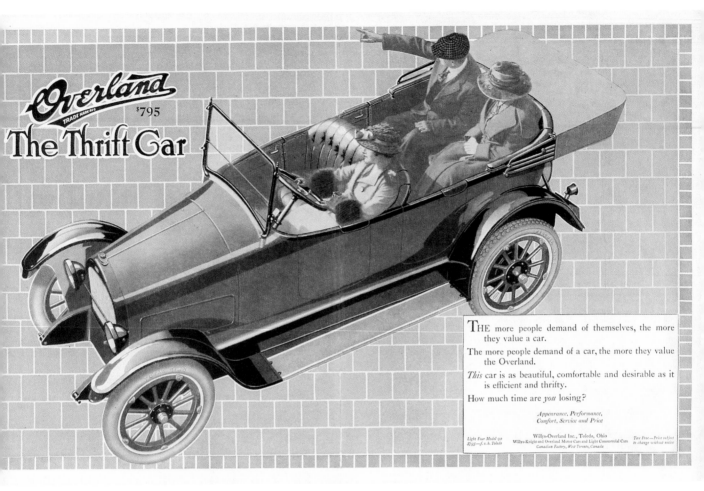

The more people demand of themselves, the more they value a car.

The more people demand of a car, the more they value the Overland.

This car is as beautiful, comfortable and desirable as it is efficient and thrifty.

How much time are *you* losing?

*Appearance, Performance,
Comfort, Service and Price*

Willys-Overland Inc., Toledo, Ohio
Willys-Knight and Overland Motor Cars and Light Commercial Cars
Canadian Factory, West Toronto, Canada

ILLUSTRATION 9

Saturday Evening Post, 1916

ILLUSTRATION 9. Indeed, it was not unusual to show women driving in the early years of automobile advertising. The intention was to demonstrate the simplicity, safety and reliability of the product. This was especially true after the invention of the self-starter by Cadillac in 1912. Finally, the difficulties and dangers of crank-starting automobiles could be avoided. An advertisement for Buick in 1916, with a pen and ink drawing reminiscent of fashion artists such as Georges Barbier, describes how motoring could be seen as a symbol of independence for privileged women, particularly significant in the context of the campaign for women's suffrage ILLUSTRATION 10. The condescending theme that women struggle with the technicalities of motoring and car maintenance was recurrent throughout the history of automobile advertising in the twentieth century.

ILLUSTRATION 10

The Sphere, 1916

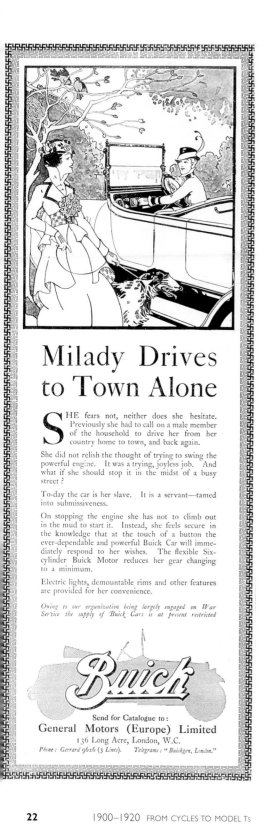

Milady Drives to Town Alone

SHE fears not, neither does she hesitate. Previously she had to call on a male member of the household to drive her from her country home to town, and back again.

She did not relish the thought of trying to swing the powerful engine. It was a trying, joyless job. And what if she should stop it in the midst of a busy street?

To-day the car is her slave. It is a servant—tamed into submissiveness.

On stopping the engine she has not to climb out in the mud to start it. Instead, she feels secure in the knowledge that at the touch of a button the ever-dependable and powerful Buick Car will immediately respond to her wishes. The flexible Six-cylinder Buick Motor reduces her gear changing to a minimum.

Electric lights, demountable rims and other features are provided for her convenience.

Owing to our organization being largely engaged on War Service the supply of Buick Cars is at present restricted

Send for Catalogue to:

General Motors (Europe) Limited

136 Long Acre, London, W.C.

Phone : Gerrard 9626 (3 Lines). Telegrams : "Buickgen, London."

The first twenty years of the twentieth century saw a shift in the aesthetics and techniques of advertising. As we have seen, much of the automobile advertising of this period focused on rather bland technical descriptions, but in January 1915, Cadillac's revolutionary advertisement, 'The Penalty of Leadership', marked a change in advertising style and attitude **ILLUSTRATION 11**. The advertisement remarkably appeared only once in the *Saturday Evening Post* but proved so legendary that the company have had requests ever since for copies of the text. Millions have so far been distributed. Even Elvis Presley had a framed copy in his office in Graceland. In late 1914, Cadillac's V8 Touring model had some defects which were damaging the company's brand image of dependability and Packard was winning the sales battle. The 'Penalty of Leadership' advertisement was a huge success and not only improved sales but helped to restore Cadillac's reputation. The stark and direct style of this advertisement focuses on the Cadillac brand rather than the cars the company was producing. In fact, there is no mention of the product at all in the large body of text. In the original publication, only a small reproduction of the Cadillac logo appeared on the border. Instead, the lofty discussion of the problems faced by leaders in society implied Cadillac's status as the leader in automobile design. The sentiments of the text captured the popular imagination and were used as inspirational and motivational narratives. Leading advertisers ever since often cite the 'Penalty of Leadership' advertisement as one of the best of all time.

THE PENALTY oF LEADERSHIP

IN EVERY FIELD OF HUMAN ENDEAVOR · HE THAT IS FIRST MUST PERPETUALLY LIVE IN THE WHITE LIGHT OF PUBLICITY ❧ WHETHER THE LEADERSHIP BE VESTED IN A MAN OR IN A MANUFACTURED PRODUCT · EMULA TION AND ENVY ARE EVER AT WORK ❧ IN ART · IN LITERATURE · IN MUSIC · IN INDUSTRY · THE REWARD AND THE PUNISHMENT ARE ALWAYS THE SAME ❧ THE REWARD IS WIDESPREAD RECOGNITION · THE PUNISHMENT FIERCE DENIAL AND DETRACTION ❧ WHEN A MAN'S WORK BECOMES A STANDARD FOR THE WHOLE WORLD IT ALSO BECOMES A TARGET FOR THE SHAFTS OF THE ENVIOUS FEW ❧ IF HIS WORK IS MERELY MEDIOCRE HE WILL BE LEFT SEVERELY ALONE ❧ IF HE ACHIEVE A MASTERPIECE · IT WILL SET A MILLION TONGUES A·WAG GING ❧ JEALOUSY DOES NOT PROTRUDE ITS FORKED TONGUE AT THE ARTIST WHO PRODUCES A COMMON PLACE PAINTING ❧ WHATSOEVER YOU WRITE · OR PAINT · OR PLAY · OR SING · OR BUILD · NO ONE WILL STRIVE TO SURPASS OR TO SLANDER YOU · UNLESS YOUR WORK BE STAMPED WITH THE SEAL OF GENIUS ❧ LONG LONG AFTER A GREAT WORK OR A GOOD WORK HAS BEEN DONE · THOSE WHO ARE DISAPPOINTED OR ENVI OUS CONTINUE TO CRY OUT THAT IT CANNOT BE DONE ❧ SPITEFUL LITTLE VOICES IN THE DOMAIN OF ART WERE RAISED AGAINST OUR OWN WHISTLER AS A MOUNTEBANK · LONG AFTER THE BIG WORLD HAD ACCLAIM ED HIM ITS GREATEST ARTISTIC GENIUS ❧ MULTITUDES FLOCKED TO BAYREUTH TO WORSHIP AT THE MUSICAL SHRINE OF WAGNER · WHILE THE LITTLE GROUP OF THOSE WHOM HE HAD DETHRONED AND DISPLACED ARGUED ANGRILY THAT HE WAS NO MUSICIAN AT ALL ❧ THE LITTLE WORLD CONTINUED TO PROTEST THAT FULTON COULD NEVER BUILD A STEAMBOAT · WHILE THE BIG WORLD FLOCKED TO THE RIVER BANKS TO SEE HIS BOAT STEAM BY ❧ THE LEADER IS ASSAILED BECAUSE HE IS A LEADER · AND THE EFFORT TO EQUAL HIM IS MERELY ADDED PROOF OF THAT LEADERSHIP ❧ FAILING TO EQUAL OR TO EXCEL · THE FOLLOWER SEEKS TO DEPRECIATE AND TO DESTROY · BUT ONLY CONFIRMS ONCE MORE THE SUPERIORITY OF THAT WHICH HE STRIVES TO SUP PLANT ❧ THERE IS NOTHING NEW IN THIS ❧ IT IS AS OLD AS THE WORLD AND AS OLD AS THE HUMAN PASSIONS ENVY · FEAR · GREED · AMBITION AND THE DESIRE TO SURPASS ❧ AND IT ALL AVAILS NOTHING ❧ IF THE LEADER TRULY LEADS HE REMAINS — THE LEADER ❧ MASTER POET · MASTER PAINTER · MASTER WORKMAN · EACH IN HIS TURN IS ASSAILED · AND EACH HOLDS HIS LAURELS THROUGH THE AGES ❧ THAT WHICH IS GOOD OR GREAT MAKES ITSELF KNOWN · NO MATTER HOW LOUD THE CLAMOR OF DENIAL ❧ THAT WHICH DESERVES TO LIVE — LIVES

ILLUSTRATION 11

Any Color so Long as it's Black, 1976

Chapter 2

1920s

Style and status

After the end of the First World War, the munitions factories were redundant and the work force which had been built up for the war effort now required other employment. In addition, the customers of the new era were ready for a change. The development of efficient mass-production during the war allowed prices to be reduced and cars were now more affordable for the professional and middle classes. Some advertising, particularly in America, even tried to encourage the two-car family **ILLUSTRATION 12**. The style of cars was changing too. Early custom-built luxury cars which appealed to the very wealthy and were designed to be chauffeur-driven were in decline. Car owners preferred to drive themselves, now that the improved technology of motoring made this easier. An advertisement for Maxwell cars from 1920 illustrates a declining fashion: children playing chauffeur and passenger in an open car **ILLUSTRATION 13**. Customers were also showing a preference for closed-bodied cars (or sedans) which would protect them from the elements and the dusty roads. In America in 1919, 90 per cent of all new cars had open bodies, but by 1929, that figure had fallen to 10 per cent (Ikuta, 1988a, p.10). Ford introduced its closed-body Model T in 1924. It was becoming more common for American car manufacturers to make their own components rather than just assembling parts. This led to an integration of components as cars began to show signs of a cohesiveness of design and a desire for individual style.

Is Your Wife Marooned During the Day?

Have you ever considered what is meant by the hundreds of cars parked in the business sections during working hours?

Most of them carried business men to work, leaving their wives and families at home, marooned because the family's one car is in daily use by the husband and father.

That is one reason why architects and builders now find that all suburban and many city homes must be provided with twin garages.

The Chevrolet Utility Coupé with Fisher Body makes an ideal extra car, especially in combination with a 5-passenger touring or sedan.

The wife finds it of every day utility for shopping, calling, taking the children to school in bad weather, etc.

Its price and upkeep are low yet the quality is high.

Chevrolet Motor Company
Division of General Motors Corporation

Detroit, Michigan

for Economical Transportation

Utility Coupé
$680
f. o. b. Flint, Mich.

Prices F. O. B. Flint, Mich.

Two Pass. Roadster	$510
Five Pass. Touring	525
Two Pass. Utility Coupe	680
Four Pass. Sedanette	850
Five Pass. Sedan	860
Light Delivery	510

There are now more than 10,000 Chevrolet Dealers and Service Stations Throughout the World.

Applications will be considered from high grade dealers in territory not adequately covered.

"Mention the Geographic— It identifies you."

ILLUSTRATION 12

National Geographic, 1923

MAXWELL

More miles per gallon *More miles on tires.*

Just as superfluous weight handicaps the heart and mind of a man, so does superfluous weight handicap the action of a motor car. Such weight kills tires,"eats up gas," kills "pep" in an engine, slows down car speed, makes repairs costly and too frequent. Maxwell has no useless weight. Special steels have been used in its construction.

They are made to Maxwell's own formulae. That is why a Maxwell is responsive, develops a high average road speed, is not tiring to drive, has a quick and sure brake action, has long "gas" and tire mileage, and why it is a stranger to the repairman. Such high efficiency wins many friendships.

Figures like these speak eloquently: 5,000 a year six years ago; 100,000 a year today; now over 400,000 in service the world over.

MAXWELL MOTOR COMPANY, INC., DETROIT, MICH.
MAXWELL MOTOR CO. OF CANADA, LTD., WINDSOR, ONTARIO
MAXWELL MOTOR SALES CORP., EXPORT DIVISION,
71 BROADWAY, NEW YORK

ILLUSTRATION 13
Saturday Evening Post, 1920

Advertising for cars was also changing. As customers demanded style and individuality, so advertising reflected the new approach. Automobile manufacturers started to employ advertising professionals and specialists to develop their campaigns to sell their cars in growing and competitive markets. There was a shift away from listing technical specifications to developing the image of the car as a symbol of status and style. This shift is illustrated by Ned Jordan's famous advertising campaign, 'Somewhere West of Laramie' which had a huge impact **ILLUSTRATION 14**. Before starting his own motor company, Edward (Ned) Jordan had been an advertising manager and a professional publicity man. He transferred

his talents to promoting his own products, and created a new style of advertising which appealed to the customer's imagination rather than just practical requirements. Jordan's Playboy model was first advertised in the *Saturday Evening Post* in 1923, and its radical approach changed automobile advertising from that point. The image, painted by the artist Fred Cole, shows a woman driving at speed and racing a cowboy in the wide open spaces of the American West. The copy evokes the freedom, adventure and fun of the motoring experience and diverts attention from the realities of technical problems and discomfort. It was also one of the first advertisements to show a moving car.

ILLUSTRATION 14

1923
The American Automobile, 1988

Somewhere West of Laramie

SOMEWHERE west of Laramie there's a broncho-busting, steer-roping girl who knows what I'm talking about. She can tell what a sassy pony, that's a cross between greased lightning and the place where it hits, can do with eleven hundred pounds of steel and action when he's going high, wide and handsome.

The truth is—the Jordan Playboy was built for her.

JORDAN

JORDAN MOTOR CAR COMPANY *Inc., Cleveland, Ohio*

The unmistakable difference in Liberty riding and driving not only adds greatly to the enjoyment of every moment spent in the car; but it also demonstrates beyond all argument, sound and enduring quality—which is the source and the foundation of that difference.

Liberty Motor Car Company, Detroit

LIBERTY SIX

ILLUSTRATION 15

Saturday Evening Post, 1920

"*Contentment*"—Absolute contentment in her motor car choice is reserved for the woman who owns a New V-63 Cadillac.

She takes special satisfaction in the safety afforded by Cadillac Four-wheel Brakes, and in the performance of the new harmonized and balanced V-Type eight cylinder engine—as smooth and quiet as it is powerful and dependable.

Each succeeding ride in the New V-63 confirms her belief in its leadership.

It is the car she desires, and the car she possesses, and therein lies the secret of her enviable motoring contentment.

CADILLAC MOTOR CAR COMPANY, DETROIT, MICH.
Division of General Motors Corporation

CADILLAC
STANDARD OF THE WORLD

Cadillac V-63 Roadster

ILLUSTRATION 16

1924

Unfortunately, this revolutionary campaign only temporarily improved the sales of Jordan cars. Indeed, the company did not withstand the impact of the Depression and closed in 1931. An advertisement for the Liberty Motor Car Company of Detroit's Liberty Six in 1920 **ILLUSTRATION 15** has an uncluttered look, using an image of a woman driving, about to take a respectable-looking man as a passenger, with copy emphasising the pleasure of motoring over the need for reliability.

Jordan, in addition to his advertising innovations, also took note of the influence of women on the automobile market. He realised that the style of cars and car advertising needed to appeal to women as well as men. In 1917, he declared that 'While men buy cars, women choose them'. By the 1920s, car marketing was no longer a matter of persuading people to buy a car, but more a matter of convincing them to replace their original car even if it was still in good working order. As David Gartman observes, culturally consumers were becoming less interested in the technology of the automobile, and more interested in the car as a symbol of status and progress (Gartman, 1994, p.62). Advertising started to concentrate on the image and style of the car. An advertisement for Cadillac from 1924 emphasises the class and beauty of the car driver, rather than the car itself. The copy also includes the word 'leadership', referring back to the famous 'Penalty of Leadership' advertisement of 1915 **ILLUSTRATION 16**.

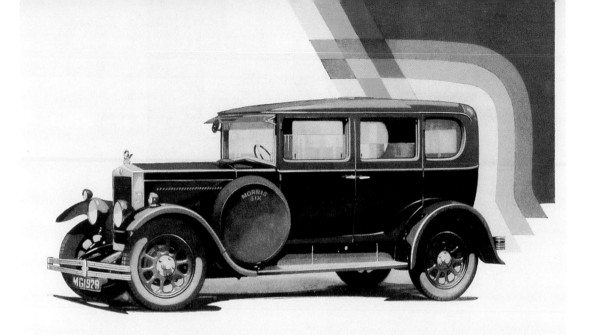

MORRIS

The Morris "Six" gives you a mile-a-minute—(*definitely*), 20 miles to the gallon —(*conservatively*), perfect comfort at all speeds—(*in reality*) and the finest Service in the world—(*unquestionably*).
In no other car can you buy more reliable or enjoyable motoring.

Coupé £365; Saloon £375, Triplex at slight extra cost. Club Coupé £399. Dunlop Tyres standard.

BUY BRITISH AND BE PROUD OF IT

ILLUSTRATION 17

Punch, 1929

ILLUSTRATION 18

Punch, 1928

ULTRA-VIOLET RAYS

Lincoln Cars are finished in cellulose.

Like everything else about the Lincoln, this lacquer has to be the finest of its kind that the world supplies.

To make sure that it is so, samples are put to test after test in the Lincoln plant.

They are even subjected to ultra-violet rays, to determine the durability of the lacquer under the hottest sun.

Costly? Fantastic? Not in the eyes of the men who make the Lincoln. No expense is too great, no test too minute, provided it can contribute one jot or one tittle to Lincoln perfection.

You see, the Lincoln is made with one aim in view—to be the finest car in the world.

40 H.P.   8 Cylinders   6 Brakes   Chassis Price £980

You may inspect the Lincoln at
16, Albemarle St., London, W.1
Dealers in all important towns and cities

LINCOLN

LINCOLN MOTOR COMPANY, DIVISION OF FORD MOTOR CO. (ENGLAND) LTD., TRAFFORD PARK, MANCHESTER

Advertisements for the British Morris Six (and the American Lincoln) show the influence of Art Deco design on advertising art **ILLUSTRATIONS 17 and 18**. The Morris Motor Company was established in 1910 by bicycle manufacturer William Morris. He opened a factory in Cowley, Oxford, and by 1924 had overtaken Ford to become Britain's biggest car manufacturer. An advertisement for Morris cars dated 1929, is unusual in that it illustrates the unglamorous but industrious production line at the Cowley factory **ILLUSTRATION 19**. Of course, at that time, most British manufacturers were urging consumers to 'Buy British' as imported goods were forming a large proportion of the market.

Despite the influence of Jordan's innovative advertisement, advertisers for automobiles still found it hard to create the impression of speed and exhilaration. Photographs and even drawings of cars in advertisements

ILLUSTRATION 19

Punch, 1929

were often static and dull. An advertisement for Daimler in 1927 tried very hard to create the movement of the car by using a directional arrow as well as flyaway clouds in the background **ILLUSTRATION 20**. Nevertheless, the image fails to make the viewer feel the 'safe speed' of the Daimler. An advertisement for Vauxhall dated 1928 successfully portrayed the efficiency of its braking system by using a stylised pen and ink drawing of the car having to stop suddenly to prevent a collision with a horse **ILLUSTRATION 21**. An unusual advertisement for the Alvis 12/50 in 1927 shows the wing-mirror view a driver might have of the Alvis trying to overtake at speed **ILLUSTRATION 22**. The Alvis 12/50 was a hugely successful sports car, capable of 75–80 miles per hour. About 350 of these Alvis models even survive in working order today. Amazingly, this is about 10 per cent of the total original production.

In America, the automobile market was booming and competition was fierce, particularly between the two giant companies of Ford and General Motors. General Motors (GM) was founded in 1908 and by the time Alfred Sloan became president in 1923 the priority was to challenge Ford's dominance. Sloan knew his company couldn't compete with Ford on price and realised that the emphasis should not be on engineering innovations, but on appearance and style. Harley Earl, a designer who had made his name customising cars for Hollywood stars, was brought in to the company and his first job was to design the La Salle in 1927 for the Cadillac

ILLUSTRATION 20

Punch, 1927

Buy British

THE CAR FOR SAFE SPEED

Daimler

SAFE SPEED under modern conditions of traffic depends entirely on the margin of power available for acceleration and hill climbing, and it is because Daimler cars are so designed as to provide the greatest possible margin at the most useful point in the speed range, that they are pre-eminently the safest fast cars on the road to-day. Anyone using a Daimler can schedule his journey from door to door at any desired average speed, and be sure of getting there on time without crawling or racing *en route*. Moreover, travelling is supremely comfortable on the Daimler, the springs and upholstery are perfectly adjusted to eliminate the effects of rough roads, the engine and transmission are smooth and silent in action, and the power-assisted brakes give absolute control over the car under all conditions.

DOUBLE-SIX
(TWO RATINGS)

5o & 3o

SIX-CYLINDER RANGE
(FOUR RATINGS)

35/120

25/85 20/70

16/55

On View at Olympia and 243 Knightsbridge

P.D. 752-2

THE DAIMLER CO. LTD. COVENTRY

ILLUSTRATION 22
1920s

ILLUSTRATION 21

The Illustrated London News, 1928

division. This was the first mass-produced car to have been designed as an integral whole by one man and was an immediate success. In addition, Sloan offered customers good trade-in deals for their old cars if they bought a new one from a range which was revamped on an annual basis. Crucially, GM also introduced the 'drive now, pay later' instalment plan. This not only promoted sales, but the company also profited from the interest charged on monthly instalments. By 1925, 65 per cent of all the company's cars were sold on the instalment plan (Ikuta, 1988a, p.10).

The Ford Company could not compete with these innovations and Henry Ford was resistant to spending large amounts on advertising or design, even regarding payment plans as immoral. Even the promotion of the Model T in 1925 at the incredibly low price of $260 could not slow the decline in sales. Production of the Model T ended in 1927. In that year 68 per cent of all the world's cars were Model T Fords.

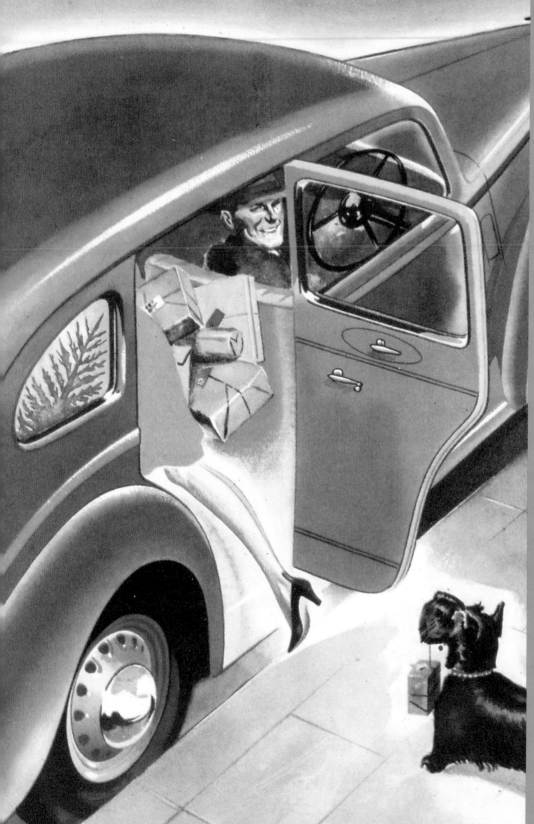

Chapter 3

1930s

Streamlining
to survive

F ollowing the Wall Street Crash, America plunged into an economic depression and much of the rest of the world soon followed. Production of automobiles in the United States dropped from over five and a half million cars in 1929 to just under one and a half million in 1932. People could no longer afford to buy cars. In particular, the sales of luxury cars declined and many manufacturers who didn't adapt their output and move to lower price markets, did not survive. Companies like Pierce-Arrow, Marmon, Stutz and Auburn-Duesenberg went out of business in the 1930s. An advertisement for Marmon in 1930 shows a vain attempt to extol the virtues of an exclusive custom-made automobile, but the company dissolved in 1933 ILLUSTRATION 23. Of course, any buyer would want to be assured by an advertisement that the company from which they bought a car would be in business a year later to provide any necessary parts. Hupmobile, for example, pointed out in its advertising that as a company it was not in debt and intended to stay in business through the Depression (Roberts, 1976, p.131). One lovely Hupmobile advertisement dated 1932 ILLUSTRATION 24 does not mention the company's financial status, but gives an indication of the technique many car-makers would adopt in order to halt their decline – the development of style.

Automobile advertising in the 1930s does not generally reflect the grim outlook of the times. Common themes included glamorous portraits of wealthy people enjoying their leisure time and images illustrating the technological

MARMON

PRESENTS A NEW CUSTOM SERIES

As a further step in its fine car program Marmon, collaborating with the finest custom builders, presents at the New York and Chicago salons and at leading Marmon establishments a new series of distinguished custom creations.

Illustrated—Marmon Grand National—Sportsman's Convertible Sedan for five passengers. Marmon Big Eight chassis. Body by Locke.

MARMON MOTOR CAR COMPANY, INDIANAPOLIS

ILLUSTRATION 23
Saturday Evening Post, 1930

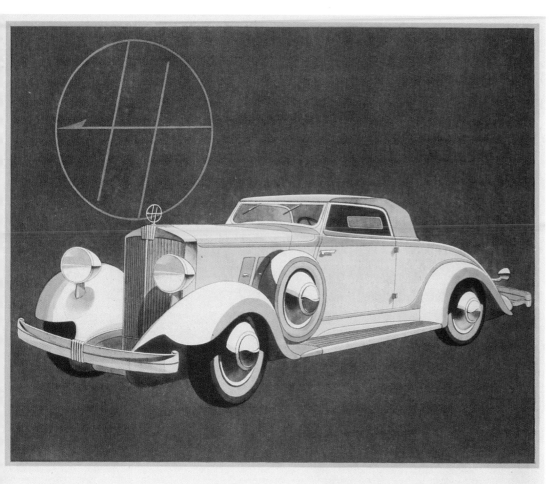

MEETING · THE · NEW · TIMES

WITH GREATER HUPMOBILE SIXES AND EIGHTS
26 MODELS . . . . $795 AND UP
AT THE FACTORY

Two views of the Cabriolet-Roadster. Note how top completely disappears, leaving just a smooth expanse of gleaming metal.

ILLUSTRATION 24

Saturday Evening Post, 1932

ILLUSTRATION 25

The Sketch, 1935

ILLUSTRATION 26

Saturday Evening Post, 1930

hopes for the future, giving the illusion of progress. The campaign for Alvis cars in Britain in the mid-1930s often depicted the upper classes at play in association with its product ILLUSTRATION 25. An advertisement for Pontiac dated 1930 uses stylised images of sailing boats to give an impression of movement, grace and freedom

ILLUSTRATION 26. General Motors used an image of carefree holidays to impress on its customers the quietness of the engine and the 'luxuriously restful' quality of a drive in the Viking Eight ILLUSTRATION 27. The image gives a persuasive message, but the tag-line 'It Grows On You' is not so convincing.

ILLUSTRATION 27

Saturday Evening Post, 1930

It Grows On You · ·

Owners insist that the Viking Eight — like all really good things — improves upon acquaintance . . . that as the months and miles go by they discover sources of satisfaction which even the first thrill of new car ownership cannot equal. ᵛ ᵛ ᵛ They say, for example, that they have found Viking's 90-degree V-type eight-cylinder engine to be truly competent in every requirement of speed, power, and acceleration — that its full-range smoothness adds to motoring pleasure. ᵛ ᵛ ᵛ They say that its beautiful body by Fisher is staunch, quiet, and luxuriously restful. That its splendidly designed chassis contributes to comfort, security, and ease of control under all conditions. That, as time goes on, the many advantages of Viking's thorough dependability become more and more apparent. ᵛ ᵛ ᵛ You can prove these things by talking to any Viking owner. ᵛ ᵛ ᵛ And you can check the basis of this satisfaction by seeing and driving the car yourself. ᵛ ᵛ ᵛ Then you will know what a truly fine automobile the Viking is . . . and you will understand why it grows on you as the miles roll by.

VIKING EIGHT

P R O D U C T   O F   G E N E R A L   M O T O R S

As manufacturers could no longer afford to invest money in technical improvements, the emphasis shifted to the development of style and appearance and the craze for 'streamlining' began. Cars started to look longer, lower and rounder in advertising illustrations and in actual car construction. For example, the wheelbase of the Chevrolet grew from 103 inches in 1923 to 109 inches in 1931

(Gartman, 1994, p.95). Mass-produced cars were made to look like high-class cars with an integrated unified appearance. There were kits available to streamline Model T Fords in order to give them the appearance of a higher-priced car. An advertisement for General Motors' Oldsmobile in 1933 illustrates the artificial elongation of the car, as well as styling details that were being introduced

Creating the New Mode for 1933 ... **BRILLIANT NEW STYLING AND PERFORMANCE AT GREATLY REDUCED PRICES**

Smart design has become a motor car essential. You can and should demand it *along with every other desirable quality*. And the combination need not be expensive. . . . Oldsmobile offers you two extremely smart, brilliant new cars —cars of balanced excellence in all the essentials—*at the lowest Oldsmobile prices in ten years*. . . . The modish new styling is partly depicted above—but only when you inspect these automobiles "in person" can you completely understand why they are hailed as *style leaders*. Tastefully and colorfully, they express the best ideas in modern motor car design. . . . Flashing speed has been a proud Oldsmobile tradition—yet the new cars are even faster.

The Six will do from 75 to 80—the Eight from 80 to 85—*actual stop-watch miles per hour*. . . . The term "smooth," when you drive one of these cars, takes on a new meaning—for the engines are scientifically balanced and cushioned in rubber mountings of entirely new design. As for "comfort," Oldsmobile has captured that desirable quality itself, whether you take it to mean easy riding or interior luxury. . . . There's comfort plus safety in the sturdy new double-drop X-type frame which greatly increases driving stability. And there's another kind of comfort in the new Fisher No-Draft Ventilation which Oldsmobile offers in all closed models. . . .

Increased body size has given both the 1933 Oldsmobiles greater roominess. And mechanical advancements have taken practically all effort out of steering, braking, and shifting gears. . . . Don't compromise, this year. Don't accept a car for any one "feature." Insist on a well-balanced combination of Style, Performance, Durability and Price. Oldsmobile offers that completeness—that real value—in its 1933 Six and Straight Eight. . . . For your convenience, the address of the nearest dealer is listed under "Oldsmobile" in the classified section of your telephone directory.

THE NEW SIX $745 · **THE NEW EIGHT $845**

ILLUSTRATION 28

Collier's Weekly, 1933

ILLUSTRATION 29

Saturday Evening Post, 1930

to enhance the streamlined look **ILLUSTRATION 28**. The chrome 'through line' fitted along the length of the car body under the windows was added to increase the appearance of length and the clever use of mirrors in the advertisement allows the viewer to see all sides of the car.

An advertisement for Fisher in 1930, body maker for General Motors, is an attempt to remind consumers not to ignore the basic construction of the car in favour of external design. It uses the image of a fashionable woman to attract male customers to what could have been a rather unglamorous illustration of a motor car body **ILLUSTRATION 29**.

ILLUSTRATION 30

Saturday Evening Post, 1932

In order to survive the depression, manufacturers were tinkering with superficial design changes rather than investing in technical and mechanical development. The policy of General Motors at the time was not to be innovative in engineering because it realised that it could make greater profits by making superficial changes to the appearance of its products. An advertisement for GM's Chevrolet range in 1932 shows how the company made subtle changes in style and colour without making substantial changes to the basic structure or engineering

ILLUSTRATION 30. Car manufacturers started to make annual changes in the look of the car in order to give the appearance of 'newness' and originality. They also invented new model names every year. As Harley Earl from General Motors said, 'our big job is to hasten obsolescence' (Gartman, 1994, p.97). Nevertheless, the major mechanical components remained generally unchanged. For example, the 'stove-bolt six' Chevrolet engine introduced in 1929 remained in production until 1954 with only minor changes (Gartman, 1994, p.96).

The 'streamlining' fashion was a visual device to give the appearance of modernity and style. Most successful new designs, however, had few aerodynamic benefits. The Chrysler Airflow, a car designed and built based on aerodynamic principles, was actually a commercial failure. The car was launched in 1934 and the body had been designed to look 'modern', but also to be aerodynamically efficient. Walter Chrysler had wanted the car marketed for the tenth anniversary of the company but only gave his engineers about fifteen months to develop it. The public rejected its stumpy, rounded front-end which appeared short in contrast to the long-bonneted cars that were becoming so popular in America at that time. An advertisement for the Airflow from 1936 has an illustration which artificially elongates the appearance of the bonnet **ILLUSTRATION 31**, but the public regarded it as looking too functional and the car sold so badly that production was halted in 1940. Despite its commercial failure, many designers were inspired by the design of the Airflow and many of its distinctive features were absorbed into later car models. The Airflow was certainly the forerunner in body design to the Volkswagen Beetle, one of the most successful and enduring of all small cars.

It is interesting that many consumer surveys taken during the 1930s revealed that car buyers claimed to want less chrome, more headroom, greater visibility and easier access for their new cars. However, the sales figures reveal that car consumers were easily seduced by the 'look' of a car and that they tended not to respond rationally

ILLUSTRATION 31

1935

Reproduced courtesy of Packard Motor Car Company

ILLUSTRATION 32

1935

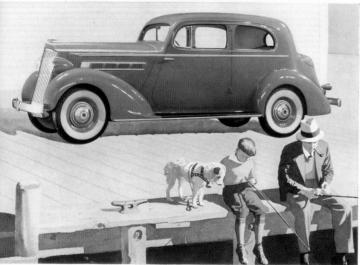

WHAT THINGS APPEAL MOST TO PEOPLE IN YOUR NEW $980 PACKARD ?

The Packard 120 Touring Coupe for Five Passengers, One of Seven Attractive Body Styles

THESE TO MEN

- Its Packard identity, even to its hub caps
- Its fine materials and longer life
- The greater precision of its parts
- Its agility in traffic, its roadability, its performance
- Its thriftiness with gas and oil
- The power of its 110 h. p. straight-eight motor
- Its Packard Angleset rear axle
- Its Safe-T-fleX front wheel suspension
- Its Servo-sealed hydraulic brakes
- Its greater freedom from lubrication and service needs
- Its low service costs
- The convenient purchase plan

THIS TO EVERYBODY

Its "fourth dimension"—the pleasure and pride of possession a Packard brings to the family who drives one.

ASK THE MAN WHO OWNS ONE

THESE TO WOMEN

- Its Packard identity, even to its hub caps
- Its beauty and simplicity of line
- The ease with which you can get in and out
- Its remarkable riding comfort
- Its handling ease
- Its unusual roominess and interior luxury
- Its effortless operation of clutch and gearshift
- Its level back seat floor, free from the usual "ridge"
- Its spacious luggage compartment
- Its individually-controlled ventilation system
- The safety of its Safety-plus body
- Its easy-operating parking brake
- Its economy of operation

PACKARD 120
$980 to $1095
List prices at factory—standard accessory group extra

when it came to purchasing a car. The car was quickly becoming a statement of status and taste.

It may be seen that as the industry focused on style, many more advertisements were directed at women. An advertisement for Packard in 1935, spells out the industry's view of the gender division of interest in cars **ILLUSTRATION 32.** In this advertisement it is declared that women would appreciate the 'beauty and simplicity of line' and the men 'the power of its 110h.p. straight-eight motor'. The Packard tag-line, 'Ask the man who owns one', was a hugely successful slogan which was used for several decades. Its message was of reliability and familiarity as well as having an element of snobbery as the 'man who owns one' was invariably depicted as someone of status and wealth. An advertisement for the Hillman Minx in Britain, dated 1938 was also possibly aimed at women as the style and image of the car is being emphasised rather than any economic or technological advantages **ILLUSTRATION 33.**

Even though automobile advertising generally tried hard to make consumers forget the economic hardships of the time, there were also adverts that promoted the economic advantages of their products. In an advertisement for Chevrolet Six from 1930 **ILLUSTRATION 34** the copy refers almost exclusively to the economy and fuel efficiency of the car. The happy customer at the petrol station is confident that his five-gallon purchase will be enough to complete his hundred mile trip home.

MINX *for* 1939 — *a still greater Success!*

AN MOTOR CAR CO. LTD. COVENTRY, *London* Showrooms & Export *Div.* : ROOTES LTD. Devonshire House, Piccadilly, W.

ILLUSTRATION 33

1936

More often, customers did not want to be reminded of their plight and responded strongly to advertising that promised a brighter future. Advertisements often featured aeroplanes which were symbols of modernity and technological achievement. An advertisement for Franklin from 1930, with an 'airplane-type engine', and an advertisement for a Ford V8 from 1934 both linked their vehicles with the speed, excitement and adventure of

ILLUSTRATION 34

Saturday Evening Post, 1930

48   THE SATURDAY EVENING POST   *June 21, 1930*

for Economical Transportation

IT'S WISE TO CHOOSE A SIX

Six-cylinder performance without added cost for gas, oil or upkeep

All over America, official registrations show that the six-cylinder car is outselling all other types by a decided margin. And every day the swing to the six in the low-price field grows steadily bigger and more impressive. For people everywhere are learning that the new Chevrolet not only gives all the advantages of six-cylinder smoothness, power, flexibility and comfort—*but does so without added cost for operation or upkeep!*

From the standpoint of gasoline and oil consumption, the new Chevrolet Six is just as economical as any other car you can buy. In a

recent officially-observed economy run, a Chevrolet six-cylinder Coach won first place over a field of 40 entries, averaging better than 20 miles to the gallon. At the finish the oil level in the crankcase was the same as at the start.

Equally impressive is Chevrolet's low cost of upkeep. Six-cylinder smoothness saves the entire car—engine, chassis and body—from the strain and wear of continuous vibration. This makes for greater dependability—longer life—and marked freedom from adjustments and repair.

No car shows a smaller expense for tires than

Buying 5 gallons of gasoline to cover a distance of 100 miles, is a common experience among owners of the Chevrolet Six

ILLUSTRATION 35

Saturday Evening Post, 1930

FLIGHT......

AIR-COOLING, LEADING AVIATION
INTO A NEW ERA, NOW SHOWS ITS
SUPREMACY IN THE AIRPLANE-TYPE
ENGINE OF THE NEW FRANKLIN—
MOST POWERFUL TYPE ENGINE BUILT

Guided by the purpose and vision which for 28 years have produced many automotive achievements, Franklin introduced, in January, America's first motor car with an AIRPLANE-TYPE ENGINE. Performance of the skies became the performance of Franklin. The flight of the graceful plane blended into the swift motion of the fleet Franklin.

With air-cooling sponsoring the most powerful type motor built, a new dynamic force enters the world of fine motor cars. Vastly different, is the performance of Franklin from any other car. The same power, stamina, speed and flexibility, which enabled Franklin's airplane-type engine to sensationally FLY AN AIRPLANE, give action to the new Franklin.

With acceleration, hill-climbing ability and speed comparable to its great power, this revolutionary motor sends thrills through you — shows you 60, 70, 80 on the speedometer,

but the lack of vibration and other ordinary speed sensations seem to say 30, 40, 50. Swiftly, smoothly, comfortably you travel at ANY speed . . . Riding is gliding.

The poise of the distant monoplane in flight suggests the grace of the new Franklin. Long, low, smart. The spirit of youth—the progressiveness of moderns are interpreted in every curve and contour. The whole ensemble is brilliantly beautiful.

See and drive the new Franklin as soon as is conveniently possible. That you will be pleased by its AIRPLANE FEEL is proved by the thousands of enthusiastic new Franklin Owners. Despite nearly doubled sales last year, sales this year are mounting higher. Franklin Automobile Company, Syracuse, N. Y.

FRANKLIN
AIR-COOLED

Reproduced courtesy of The H.H. Franklin Museum/Foundation

ILLUSTRATION 36

Punch, 1934

ILLUSTRATION 37

1939

V-8 SALOON DE LUXE (2 DOORS), NEWLY REDUCED PRICE, £220, AT WORKS, DAGENHAM

A new V-8 finds few equals on the road, irrespective of price. Its performance is dazzling, whether you like most the speed and acceleration that its powerful V-8 engine and low power-to-weight ratio give it, the safety of its powerful brakes and light, positive steering, the comfort of its suspension, or its surprising silence.

Drive a new V-8 yourself! Your nearest Ford Dealer will gladly let you try one over a route of your own choice. Then investigate costs, and learn for how little you can enjoy this thrilling motor car.

The action of Ford transverse springs is like the smooth, gliding flight of a bird. The wings (or spring tips) move, while the body remains steady

OR COMPANY LIMITED, DAGENHAM, ESSEX.   SHOWROOMS : 88 REGENT STREET, LONDON, W.1

Hupmobile's Air-line beauty foretells *true* Air-line performance

"The efficiency of anything that is designed for speed," engineers say, "is in direct relationship to its beauty." The truth of that statement is apparent the minute you see the new Hupmobile. When you enter this beautiful Aero-dynamic car, you will realize immediately that its direct, flowing, graceful lines can mean but one thing . . . superior performance and efficiency.

But when you drive this new car and its clean air-lines cleave through the wind at effortless high speed . . .

when you relax to the flight-like riding qualities made possible by its "coördinated suspension" and the side-sway eliminator pioneered by Hupmobile two years ago . . . then and only then will you truly know that Hupp's beauty is the sign of a new day in motoring.

There is a thrill in seeing the new Aero-dynamic Hupmobile. But the real thrill is your first ride in this ultra-modern car. We hope that you will accept your dealer's invitation for that ride today!

HUPMOBILE PRICES
127-inch wheelbase,
6-passenger Sedan $1245
121-inch wheelbase,
6-passenger Sedan $1095
117-inch wheelbase,
Four-door Sedan $795
117-inch wheelbase,
Coupe with rumble seat $795
Prices f.o.b. factory . . . tax and special equipment extra.

AERO-DYNAMIC
Hupmobile

VISIT HUPMOBILE'S EXHIBIT AT THE CHICAGO WORLD'S FAIR (TRAVEL & TRANSPORT BUILDING). DRIVE AMERICA'S MOST MODERN CAR IN A THRILLING SPECTACULAR TEST

aeroplane technology ILLUSTRATIONS 35 and 36. A stylised image used for a Hupmobile advertisement from 1939, presented a dramatically elongated impression of an airship as a symbol of modernity and streamlined invention ILLUSTRATION 37. This image also illustrates the adventurousness that advertising companies were attempting in illustration style and advertising design. An advertisement for the Ford V8 in Britain in 1933 is brave enough not to show a full image of the car ILLUSTRATION 38. The advert shows a seemingly irrelevant but relaxing and colourful river scene with only a suggestion of what is being sold. The small image of the car radiator with the V8 logo, which was becoming well-known by this time, tempts potential buyers to find out more.

ENDURING CHARM

A postcard will secure for you a copy
of the V-8 Catalogue, describing and
illustrating a remarkable motor car.

FORD MOTOR COMPANY LIMITED
DAGENHAM, ESSEX   •   Showrooms   88   REGENT   STREET,   LONDON.   W.1

ILLUSTRATION 38

Punch, 1933

An advertisement for Cadillac from 1939 shows the influence of Modernist architecture on advertising artists. This advertisement emphasises not only the size of the Cadillac Sixty-Two, 'the newest car in the world', but by linking it with the strong horizontal lines of innovative contemporary architecture, the illusion of 'newness' and modernity is also achieved **ILLUSTRATION 39**. A dramatically stylised image used for an advertisement for Pontiac in 1935 hides the faces of the driver and passenger, but suggests their wealth and status by illustrating them in tailored suits and driving gloves. Their power is also suggested by the unusual way the car is presented face-on to the viewer indicating force, intimidation and dominance **ILLUSTRATION 40**.

ILLUSTRATION 39

Esquire, 1939

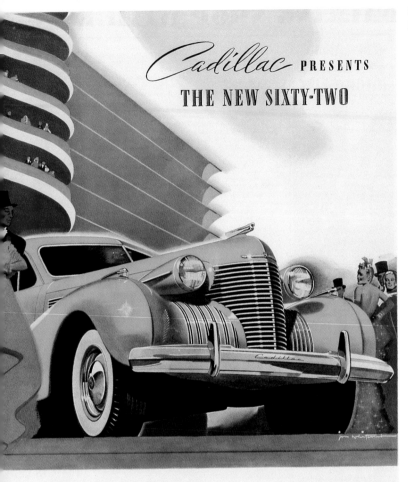

Cadillac PRESENTS

THE NEW SIXTY-TWO

» » » » » THE NEWEST CAR IN THE WORLD

THE NEW THINGS in motor cars come first from Cadillac. Witness the new Cadillac Sixty-Two, which introduces a wholly new idea of how a motor car should look and act. It's not just a new car—*it's the newest car in the world.* ¶ From its beautiful radiator to its torpedo-shaped rear deck, the Sixty-Two is a striking creation. It is easily America's most beautiful motor car. ¶ And its performance is equally new and exhilarating. Cadillac performance has always stood alone—but the Sixty-Two has a number of qualities that are uniquely its own, even among Cadillacs. ¶ You'll like this car. Better go see it right now, and make certain of early delivery.

While you're about it, see, too, the new Cadillac-Fleetwood Sixty Special—the brilliantly restyled 1940 version of "America's most imitated car."

A GENERAL MOTORS VALUE

ILLUSTRATION 40

1935

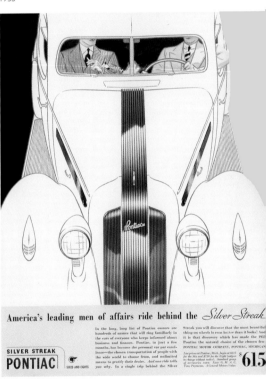

America's leading men of affairs ride behind the *Silver Streak*

SILVER STREAK
PONTIAC SIXES AND EIGHTS

$615

The illusions created by the motor industry to mask the miseries of the depression also disguised the inevitable approach of war.

Chapter 4

1940s

'There's a Ford in your future'

When the Second World War started, it effectively ended the production of civilian motor vehicles in Europe. Soon after the attack on Pearl Harbour and the entry of the United States into the war at the end of 1941, production ended there too. Car manufacturers again profited from converting their output to munitions and vehicles for the armed forces. General Motors started to build shells, bombs, fuses and anti-aircraft guns. Ford was mass-producing bomber aircraft. In Britain, Alvis helped Rolls-Royce with the production of engines for aircraft and Rootes, the company responsible for the production of the Hillman, Humber and Sunbeam marques, built a huge factory near Coventry in 1940 to build military aircraft such as the Bristol Blenheim and the heavy bomber, the Handley Page Halifax.

During the war, car manufacturers doubled their productive capacity. Even though during this time they were not marketing their products to the general public, many companies continued to produce printed advertisements. They wanted to ensure that the public not only valued their contribution to the war effort, but also that customers would remember their brands when civilian car production resumed after the war was won.

Daimler was producing armoured cars and an advertisement from 1943 celebrates the victory of the Allies against the Germans in Tunisia **ILLUSTRATION 41**.

Victory Parade, Tunis, May 20th, 1943

Daimler
goes to war

ILLUSTRATION 41

The Tatler and Bystander, 1943

FULL STEAM AHEAD!

These are days of action — momentous days. This is not the time to recall past achievements — stern, vigorous and constant endeavour for our Nation must be the order of the day. In Mr. Herbert Morrison's words, we must all " *Go to it*."

In that task Ford shoulders its share. The vast resources — human and mechanical — of the great Dagenham factory, are on urgent National work — to the utmost.

    •   •   •

We will return some time to telling the fine story of Ford engineering genius — just as we shall return to the making of ever-better cars for the pleasant highways of peace-time. Meanwhile . . .

FORD MARCHES ON

ILLUSTRATION 42

Picture Post, 1940

An advertisement by Ford in 1940 spelt out its own contribution to 'National work' and promised a return to producing 'ever-better cars' **ILLUSTRATION 42**. In America, General Motors overtly presented an image of revenge for the attack by the Japanese **ILLUSTRATION 43**. The illustration depicts the destruction of Japanese cities and factories by American bombers. The company enhanced its patriotic image by encouraging the viewer to buy war bonds. An advert for Plymouth dated 1944 also reminds the viewer that the company was still operating and the image reinforced the idea of industriousness and purpose **ILLUSTRATION 44**.

Pay-off for Pearl Harbor!

Three years ago, the sneak attack on Pearl Harbor found America unprepared to defend its rights. Yet, even at that early date, Cadillac was in its third year of building aircraft engine parts for military use. Today we look hopefully forward to the time when this important contribution to America's air power will pay off in such a scene as that illustrated above.

For more than five years we have been working toward that end. Back in 1939, we started building precision parts for Allison—America's famous liquid-cooled aircraft engine—used to power such potent fighters as the Lightning, the Warhawk, the Mustang, the Airacobra and the new Kingcobra.

In addition to our work for Allison, which has included more than 57,000,000 man-hours of precision production—we assisted Army Ordnance Engineers in designing the M-5 Light Tank and the M-8 Howitzer motor carriage, and have produced them in quan-

tities. Both are powered by Cadillac engines, equipped with Hydra-Matic transmissions.

We are now building other weapons which utilize some of our Cadillac peacetime products. We can't talk about all of them yet—but we are confident they will prove significant additions to Allied armor.

Every Sunday Afternoon . . . GENERAL MOTORS SYMPHONY OF THE AIR—NBC Network

CADILLAC MOTOR CAR DIVISION  GENERAL MOTORS CORPORATION

 LET'S ALL
BACK THE ATTACK
BUY WAR BONDS

ILLUSTRATION 43

1944

ILLUSTRATION 44

Life, 1944

ILLUSTRATION 45

1944

A fine example of the illustrator Dean Cornwell's[1] work is shown in an advertisement for Fisher Bodies, a division of General Motors **ILLUSTRATION 45**. Cornwell was well known in the 1940s for his patriotic war posters and illustrations for advertising. This image dramatically and theatrically evokes the heroism, not only of the pilot, but of the engineer who works through the night to build instruments for navigation. The war was an opportunity for automobile companies to present themselves as forces for the national good.

In 1945, Ford started to use a new advertising company, the well-established J. Walter Thompson Agency. The advertisements started to feature the image of a crystal ball held behind the Ford logo with a slogan, 'There's a Ford in your future' **ILLUSTRATION 46**. The message of

1   Dean Cornwell 1892–1960, illustrator
and mural painter, born in Kentucky.

THE CAR OF THE YEAR...THE ONE AND ONLY NEW CAR IN ITS FIELD!

Inside, outside, the Ford Forty-Niner is completely new! "Dream car" silhouette . . . 10 new colors that keep that "Showroom Complexion". . . lots of room for six . . ."Picture Window" Visibility all around! New springs, front and rear . . . new "Magic Action" King-Size Brakes . . . choice of two new engines, V-8 or Six. Savings up to 10% on gasoline—up to 25% with Overdrive!* See "The Car of the Year" at your Ford Dealer's today!

*Optional at extra cost

White Side Wall tires available at extra cost

New "Mid Ship" Ride in level center section where the going's smoothest . . . plus new "Hydra-Coil" Front Springs, "Para-Flex" Rear Springs built parallel to the frame. Yes, in the new Ford you get the ride of the year!

There's a NEW *Ford* in your future

FORD

ILLUSTRATION 46

Saturday Evening Post, 1948

this new campaign epitomised the immediate post-war era of car advertising. When car production resumed after the war, even though most of the models were the same as pre-war models, companies were keen to give the impression of looking to the future and promising a new beginning. In Britain, an advertisement for Lanchester in June 1945, expresses a sense of excitement and anticipation for the new, peacetime products

ILLUSTRATION 47

The Illustrated London News, 1945

WHAT WILL IT BE LIKE . . .

THAT POST-WAR CAR OF 19—? It must embody all those striking advances in technical achievement which will result from wartime research and experience. It must show a new perfection of design and workmanship. It must be absolutely reliable, while combining higher speed with lower running cost. It must give maximum comfort. The post-war LANCHESTER will offer all this and something more . . . an innate quality of distinction, created by the individual work of experienced craftsmen. A car well worth waiting for . . . a car which crowns performance with personality.

BY APPOINTMENT

LANCHESTER

ILLUSTRATION 47. In this advertisement, the car itself cannot be seen. We only see two men, eagerly awaiting a sight of the new car coming around the corner. Similarly, an advertisement for Wolseley in 1946 uses the line, 'Pride of Ownership', and depicts a couple encompassing their new, valuable possessions with promise of a peaceful and prosperous future ILLUSTRATION 48.

In America, even before the end of the war, an advertisement for Pontiac encourages owners to look after their

ILLUSTRATION 48

The Illustrated London News, 1946

ILLUSTRATION 49

Saturday Evening Post, 1944

"Gee! you surely took care
of my Pontiac!"

When the boys dream about coming home —somewhere in the vision there's an image of those cars they left behind them.

And, naturally, they see them as they left them . . . with the same old zip and pickup, the same shiny hoods and fenders.

If you have charge of a "service star" car, you have a special obligation—to minimize the wear and tear of the months

and the miles. You owe it to him, as well as to the war effort, to keep it looking and running at its very best.

Your Pontiac dealer will gladly help you with this vital job. He services all makes of cars—and his facilities are the finest obtainable. He has specialized equipment —specially trained mechanics—and uses only high quality parts for replacement. See him regularly.

PONTIAC **MOTOR DIVISION**
General Motors Corporation

Every Sunday Afternoon . . . GENERAL MOTORS SYMPHONY OF THE AIR — NBC Network

cars while their soldier owners are at war: 'you owe it to him, as well as to the war effort' **ILLUSTRATION 49**. American car-makers had trouble meeting the pent-up demand once the war was over. Suburbs grew, industries and job opportunities boomed and a nationwide programme to build interstate highways was being planned. An advertisement for General Motors in 1947 **ILLUSTRATION 50** demonstrates the blurring of the boundaries between urban and rural life by pointing out the difficulty in differentiating between the city girl and the country girl! By the end of the decade, the sales of new cars reached an all-time record of just under five million a year. Advertising reflected this positive image of the future. In advertisements cars were depicted driving on newly built bridges, dams and motorways. In an advertisement for the 'Futuramic' Oldsmobile in 1946, the car is shown being driven over a new dam with roads on two levels **ILLUSTRATION 51**. A British advertisement for the Rootes Group in 1946 similarly shows cars being driven freely on wide dual carriageways and bridges

ILLUSTRATION 50

1947

ILLUSTRATION 51

1949

PROBLEM:

Find the Farmer's Daughter

no sure way of telling Laurel Ann city cousin.

ys country girls and city girls look ess alike and think alike — and the nd the radio aren't the only reasons.

not true years ago, when cars were roads were bad and the farm was vay from town.

n then companies like General Motors king ways to find new customers. st way seemed to be to make their better — more useful to more people.

by year, they plowed back sizable of their earnings into im-designs, steady research, ficient factories — all the nat make progress.

y year cars got better. ept step. Buses and trucks

In HENRY J. TAYLOR, Monday and Friday A, over more than 500 Mutual stations cost to coast. Hear him!

Suburbs have spread. Great industries have grown. Jobs have multiplied.

At General Motors alone the total annual pay roll has been increased more than sixteen-fold in the last 29 years. During the same time the people who own GM, the stockholders — today numbering more than 425,000 — have received only about 7½¢ out of each dollar of sales.

came. And the United States became really united in its ways of living and learning and doing business.

Now Laurel Ann rides to the same stores, the same movies, the same kind of schools as her friends in town. But that isn't all that has happened.

Only because General Motors and companies like it have prospered — and thus been able to improve their products — have so many people benefited in so many places.

So it seems clear that *all the people* profit when a business prospers.

"MORE AND BETTER THINGS FOR MORE PEOPLE"

GENERAL MOTORS

THE PEOPLE PROFIT WHEN A BUSINESS PROSPERS

· GMC TRUCK & COACH · GM DIESEL · **CHEVROLET · PONTIAC · OLDSMOBILE · BUICK · CADILLAC · BODY BY FISHER** · DELCO · UNITED MOTORS SERVICE · AC SPARK PLUGS ·

Powered by the new "*ROCKET*" engine!

Futuramic "98" 2-Door Sedan with "Rocket" engine, "Hydra-Matic Drive standard equipment on Series "98" and "88," optional at extra cost on "76." White sidewall tires optional at extra cost.

If only *you* were at that wheel . . . if only *you* were driving this new Futuramic Oldsmobile! Then you'd know what we mean by "Rocket" Engine power! Then you'd appreciate this completely new high-compression action that words just can't describe. "Silence" won't convey your wonder at the hushed "Rocket" quietness. "Smoothness" doesn't do justice to the perfect teamwork of Hydra-Matic Drive* and the "Rocket". And "response" doesn't begin to say what it means to ride this full, flowing wave of power. It's a new way to travel! It's an air-borne sensation that you must *try to believe!* And now you can do so in the new, lower-priced Futuramic "88"—as well as the big, luxurious "98." So see your Oldsmobile dealer *soon*—drive his special "Rocket" demonstrator—discover *The New Thrill!*

The New Thrill

FUTURAMIC **OLDSMOBILE**

ILLUSTRATION 52

1946

First on the roads of the New World

Humber, Hillman, Sunbeam - Talbot . . . their history is the history of motoring. The engineers who build them, the designers who fashion them, have contributed to motoring many of its finest features. Tried and tested in two wars, proved in every continent, their past proclaims their future. They will be first on the roads of the new world.

HUMBER
HILLMAN
SUNBEAM-TALBOT

PRODUCTS OF THE ROOTES GROUP

ILLUSTRATION 52. Both of these advertisements portray products as being part of forward-looking, post-war construction.

Willys is an example of an American car company that took best advantage of the marketing opportunities of war ILLUSTRATION 53. The 'Jeep', the general purpose quarter-ton truck was created by the American Bantam Car Company in 1940 and the design was then licensed to Ford and Willys-Overland because the demand was greater than Bantam could supply. During the war, Willys produced over 350,000 Jeeps and Ford produced around 280,000. The car was cited by President Eisenhower as one of the most important items of military hardware in the Allied victory. After the war, Ford relinquished its interest in producing Jeeps and Willys took over sole production. Willys put into production the Jeepster, the first four-wheel-drive passenger car for the

ILLUSTRATION 53

1943

A salute to the brave and vitally important U. S. Army Engineers

ENGINEERS BRIDGE NEW GUINEA RIVER UNDER FIRE

WITH JEEPS FROM WILLYS-OVERLAND

AN American army engineer who had just returned from active service in New Guinea, described this exciting incident. From his vivid word picture Mr. James Sessions, famous war artist, painted the illustration above. The army engineer says it is "amazingly realistic." This is the story:

* * *

"It was one of those hot, sweaty days in the jungles of New Guinea. Our fighters had driven the Japs back all the day before, through tangled jungle and over rocky escarpments.

"They were just approaching a ponton bridge which we engineers had put across the river under cover of a typical morning mist, when an order came from our commanding officer for a flanking movement.

"A force was to cross the river about two miles downstream. And that meant another bridging job for the engineers, *in broad daylight.*

"With our combat guard, our trusty Jeeps from Willys-Overland and bridge equipment, we covered those two miles in nothing flat.

"The river was depth-tested, and a crossing point was selected. Then began the fastest bridge-laying operation I ever expect to see.

"We had hardly begun when we heard planes overhead and we all knew we were in for a job, *under fire.*

"The big pontons were quickly inflated. A Willys-built Jeep hauled them into the water, one by one. Another Jeep nudged them into position and held them against the current. Skilled engineering hands secured the pontons and laid the flooring.

"Meanwhile, other Jeeps had ploughed across the river and their crews were blasting away at Jap planes that were continually bombing and strafing the operation.

"With the engineers and their 'mighty' Willys-built Jeeps working as a perfect team, we laid that emergency bridge in record time.

"The last floor plank was hardly in place, when our flanking troops came into view. They crossed the bridge and the attack moved forward as planned—to give the Japs another helluva beating!"

* * *

We salute the brave and efficient U.S. Army Engineers. They are the advance guard and trouble shooters who pave the way for our fighting forces, *wherever the going is tougher than tough.*

It was Willys-Overland's fine staff of engineers who, in close cooperation with Army Service Forces, created and perfected the Jeep. This unit of America's modern motorized army is procured and maintained by the Ordnance Department for our fighting forces—throughout the world.

The world-renowned "Go-Devil" engine that drives all Jeeps with such power, speed, flexibility and economy, is an exclusive Willys-Overland development.

U. S. ARMY JEEP

WILLYS

MOTOR CARS   TRUCKS AND JEEPS

AMERICAR—the People's Car

THE GO-DEVIL ENGINE—power-heart of WILLYS CARS and all JEEPS

ILLUSTRATION 54

1948

now comes a dream of a car . . . a daring, fun-loving dream,

realized in steel and chrome . . . to thrill those "special" kinds of

people who tire of the ordinary and always seek the uncommon:

meet the **Jeepster**

The fleet, low-slung lines of the Jeepster tell you in advance: "Here is a companion for carefree moments".
Come, sit under the wheel, and deny if you can the desire to roam new roads with the Jeepster.
Take off from the crowded highway, the mob is not for you . . . Seek the unspoiled spots and strange scenes.
Go with the wind, commanding the power of the mighty 'Jeep' engine. And soon, you'll settle back in the seat with a smile . . . For this is *fun!*

If you're headed for the shore, the mountains, or a brisk turn on the boulevard, your spirits will run high with the Jeepster.
Vacation journey or workaday errand alike are less tiring, because there's a lift to your spirits.
Leave the more formal cars to more formal people.
You'll drive the Jeepster for the sheer joy of driving, of going somewhere, with laughter in your heart and a song on your lips.
Meet the Jeepster now, at Willys-Overland dealers.

WILLYS-OVERLAND MOTORS, TOLEDO, OHIO, U.S.A. • MAKERS OF AMERICA'S MOST USEFUL VEHICLES

general public. This car was one of the first of what now is known as the SUV (Sport Utility Vehicle, also known as '4×4') **ILLUSTRATION 54**.

While post-war sales were booming in America, Britain was still suffering the effects of war restrictions. Petrol rationing continued until 1950 and strict rationing of food was still in force for some items well into the 1950s. Britain could no longer afford to buy American or other foreign cars. Import restrictions were introduced to attempt to improve the country's balance of payments and manufacturers were encouraged to export as much as possible in order to earn foreign currency. The Government allocated steel to manufacturers according to the proportion of production they exported. In 1950, Britain exported 75 per cent of all cars produced. An advertisement for the Nuffield Organisation from 1948 promotes the company as a major, patriotic exporter whose overseas trade allowed the country to import essential food **ILLUSTRATION 55**.

By the end of the decade, while the British and Europeans were struggling to produce and sell cars in their own markets, in America, the design and advertising of automobiles signified the booming prosperity, development and promise of the post-war years. Americans were looking forward to the new technological age and cars would be the ultimate symbols of that optimism and confidence.

ILLUSTRATION 55

The Illustrated London News, 1948

SHOPPING WITH A CAR

The Nuffield Organization goes shopping for Britain overseas. Every year scores of thousands of vehicles made by Nuffield Organization firms are hoisted aboard ship, carried across the sea, and sold to people who value British engineering skill. As a result of these exports, Britain is able to fill her national shopping basket with food-stuffs. When you eat your morning cereal and toast, cut into the Sunday joint, peel an orange or eat an egg, you are enjoying something that has been in part paid for by the hard work and craftsmanship of 20,000 Nuffield workers.

MORRIS

WOLSELEY

RILEY

M.G.

MORRIS-COMMERCIAL

**THE
NUFFIELD ORGANIZATION**

Chapter 5

1950s

The bold new
generation

The 1950s was known as the 'Golden Age' of the American car industry. Car sales rose with the increase in prosperity and the long, wide, tail-finned, convertible vehicle became the symbol of America's superpower status. Even in Britain, car ownership rose by 250 per cent between 1951 and 1961. Advertising of the period reflected not only the relief that post-war austerity was coming to an end, but also the hope encouraged by the dynamic vibrancy of changes in society and the economy.

The first appearance of the iconic tail fin was in the 1948 Cadillac. This was the beginning of the widespread use of military and aeronautical references in American automobile design. As the Cold War took hold on the American psyche, these symbols proliferated to reinforce the public's feeling of security in the technological dominance of their country. The 1950 Studebaker Commander was designed with a circular chrome feature on the front which was reminiscent of the new jet engines that were used in combat aircraft **ILLUSTRATION 56**. An advertisement for Chrysler in 1955, associates its products with the technology and power of

White sidewall tires and wheel trim rings extra cost

Studebaker again amazes America!

A great new V-8
1951 STUDEBAKER
COMMANDER

New peaks of power! New driving thrills!
A real gas saver! Needs no premium fuel!

*Studebaker Automatic Drive gives you
truly marvelous "no clutch-no gearshift" motoring
Available at extra cost*

© The Studebaker Corporation, South Bend 27, Indiana, U. S. A.

ILLUSTRATION 56

1951

ILLUSTRATION 57

The New Yorker, 1955

the military jet. The use of the word 'forward' and the vehicles' arrangement, so as to appear to be pointing towards the future, evoke optimism and faith in progress **ILLUSTRATION 57**.

Advertisements frequently used words like 'power', 'mighty' and 'bold', emphasising the feeling of American superiority at that time. Correspondingly, the power of the average engine increased from 110 horsepower in 1946 to 180 horsepower in 1956 (Gartman, 1994, p.155). Some companies still relied on the quality of illustrators and more sophisticated advertising techniques to promote their products, such as a 1951 advertisement for Plymouth with an illustration by Norman Rockwell of an excited family anticipating the arrival of their new car **ILLUSTRATION 58**; but generally, American car advertising followed the common theme of progress and forward-thinking.

"Oh, Boy! It's Pop with a new *PLYMOUTH!*"

ILLUSTRATION 59

The Illustrated London News, 1951

In Britain, despite the end of petrol rationing in 1950, car designers did not attempt to reproduce the long, wide, gas-guzzling American models. The Festival of Britain in 1951 marked a new beginning of the desire to create identifiable British designs to promote British products internationally. An advertisement for Austin in 1951 uses the typographic and illustrative design style of the Festival to promote the company as a representative of successful British exporters **ILLUSTRATION 59**.

British manufacturers were keen to show that they could market distinctive British products such as the Morris Minor which was launched in 1948 and was to become one of Britain's best-selling cars. By 1961, a million had been made and production continued until 1970. The car was designed by Sir Alec Issigonis who later became famous for the design of the Mini, but was most proud of his work on the Morris Minor. He considered it to be a vehicle that combined many of the luxuries and conveniences of a good motor car at a price suitable for the average working man's pocket **ILLUSTRATION 60**. Nevertheless, an advertisement for the Morris from 1952 associates the car with more wealthy members of society by portraying it with fox-hunters **ILLUSTRATION 61**. However, the car was affordable and crossed class barriers. Advertising during the 1950s often pandered to snobbery and status awareness. An advertisement for Austin in 1958 portrays an obviously wealthy family waving goodbye to its young boys who are clearly going

ILLUSTRATION 60

Punch, 1954

ILLUSTRATION 61

Country Life Annual, 1952

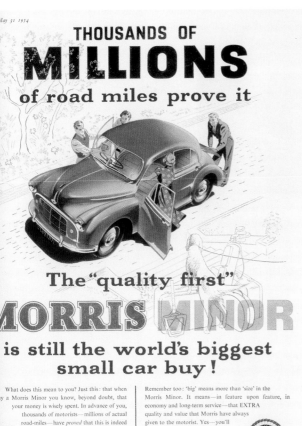

ILLUSTRATION 62

Country Life Annual, 1958

TOP CAR IN THE MIDDLE PRICE BRACKET—

The new Austin A.55

Its sleek contours alone tell you that the A.55 is something unprecedented in its price class—it proves that the solid family car need not be stolid. When you put your foot to the accelerator, that tells the same story. For the 1½ litre engine is raring to go, and makes light of the heaviest going. What's more, its high-compression ratio means you get maximum engine efficiency with minimum fuel consumption. Then the longer you live with an A.55 the more you learn to value it. A constant boon in traffic are its panoramic windscreen and rear window. Going on a trip, you bless its bigness. It lets five people stretch their legs at ease, has an outsize boot, and extra wide shelf-space for odds and ends. Every time you ride in it, you appreciate its comfort, its quiet, its luxurious fittings, its easy handling. Take it how you like, standard or de luxe, with or without Manumatic gearchange, or overdrive, in one- or two-tone colour schemes, the Austin A.55 is the finest medium price car in the world. Price: from £538 plus £270. 7s. purchase tax.

Buy **AUSTIN** and be proud of it

THE AUSTIN MOTOR COMPANY LIMITED, LONGBRIDGE, BIRMINGHAM

off by train to boarding school **ILLUSTRATION 62**. Car owners were aware that their purchase was a very public statement of their status and prosperity and responded well to suggestions that certain models were associated with more prosperous classes.

Another very popular car of this period in Britain was the Ford Zephyr **ILLUSTRATION 63**. The advertising emphasised the styling of the car by associating it with high fashion in clothing. Later models did have American-style tail fins and a proliferation of chrome detail. The Zephyr gained a high profile after the popular television series *Z-Cars* which was named after the model which was commonly used by police forces around the country. The Ford Zodiac in 1959 also associated itself with high fashion in its advertising. The advertisement seems to give

Ford ☆☆☆☆☆ Motoring

BY APPOINTMENT MOTOR
VEHICLE MANUFACTURERS TO
THE LATE KING GEORGE VI
FORD MOTOR COMPANY LTD.

Zephyr

Fashion's newest favourite—the 'Zephyr-look' about your car. But it isn't fair to judge the lovely Zephyr on its fine good-looks alone. There's *so* much more to it . . . the lightest-touch controls, the exciting power of it, the sheer comfort of it! The Zephyr—the Monte Carlo Rally winner—is *so* far ahead!

Dress and hat by *Ronald Paterson*

ILLUSTRATION 63

Vogue, 1953

ILLUSTRATION 64
1959

Dress by John Cavanagh

partner in perfection

Gay and delightful Nasturtium will be your first
fashion choice this year . . . and among your accessories
none could be more appropriate or more flattering
than the brilliant, sleek-and-handsome Zodiac Automatic,
today's fashion leader for smarter, safer motoring.

 *automatically sets the fashion*

Better looking than ever with delightful
new colours

ILLUSTRATION 65

Vogue, 1959

Velox and Cresta by Vauxhall

How very effectively good colour sets off modern design! These delightful new Vauxhall colours make the 1959 Velox and Cresta better looking than ever. And the new upholstery designs, beautifully finished in attractive shades, complete the colour harmony. Good to look at, a delight to drive and superbly engineered in every way, the Velox and Cresta are the most outstanding six-cylinder models of today. Ask your local Vauxhall dealer to show you how and why in a demonstration drive.

New colours
(as shown)
HAVEN BLUE
IMPERIAL IVORY
LAUREL GREEN
SILVER GREY
ROYAL BLUE
CHARCOAL GREY
ROYAL GLOW

Everyone drives better in a Vauxhall

Velox £655 plus £328.17s. PT (£983.17s.) · Cresta £715 plus £358.17s. PT (£1,073.17s.)

Vauxhall Motors Limited · Luton · Beds

prominence to the fashion illustration for John Cavanagh, a London couturier **ILLUSTRATION 64**. An advertisement for Vauxhall in 1958 illustrated a new interest in the styling and particularly the colour of some British cars. The image shows women choosing their car 'colour harmony' in the same way they would choose curtain fabric, and the bright pink, tail-finned car behind them reflects the influence of American dream cars. Nevertheless, the class-resonant colour names are very un-American: 'Royal Glow', 'Imperial Ivory' and 'Royal Blue' **ILLUSTRATION 65**.

Although many of the car advertisements at this time seemed to be directed at the female market, the indications are that most cars were purchased by men in the 1950s. It is likely that, although they may have denied it, men were as much attracted by the 'look' of a car as by its mechanical features. As David Gartman argues, macho pride may have prevented men from admitting that they would want a beautiful car that was easy to drive (Gartman, 1994, p.167). Advertising ostensibly directed at women would have appealed to men too.

ILLUSTRATION 66

1958

ILLUSTRATION 67

1953

DAN RUBIN

Only 7,500 Americans can get a new Jaguar this year . . .

You just can't mass produce a superb car like the new Jaguar XK150 Roadster. Witness the painstaking workmanship, the clean, smooth-flowing lines, the sports car simplicity. This newest Jaguar is the proud inheritor of Jaguar's racing traditions. Yet roominess, luxury and ease of handling make it the road car sans pareil.

In case you need an excuse to buy a Jaguar:

New features – *New* 4-wheel disc brakes, *New* one-piece wind screen, roll-up windows, convertible top. But the XK150 and XK150S retain all the Jaguar qualities connoisseurs cherish.

Performance – The famous Jaguar engine provides quiet surging power for starts and safe passing. The Jaguar suspension system prevents roll, pitching, wavering.

Resale Value – You get unbelievably high trade-in because Jaguar, the finest car of its class in the world, stands up for thousands of miles beyond expected "normal" standards.

THE BEST CAR IN THE WORLD

ILLUSTRATION 68

The Illustrated London News, 1954

Jaguar was one British make of car that was making an impact in America. The XK120 sports car was launched in 1948 in post-war Britain, with a 3.4 litre engine of 160 horsepower, which was previously unheard of, especially in a country where petrol was still rationed. The power and design caught the imagination of the rich and famous in Hollywood: Humphrey Bogart and Clark Gable were customers. An advertisement for one of its successors from 1958, the XK150, appeared in American magazines and certainly Jaguar helped to revive the market for luxury imported cars **ILLUSTRATION 66**.

Rolls-Royce used the slogan 'The Best Car in the World' from the date the company was established in 1906. It was well known for creating memorable and unconventional advertising that used the company's recognisable symbols and its familiar slogan to catch the eye. A black and white line-drawn advertisement from 1953 strikingly illustrates only a small part of the car: the familiar radiator. Of course, the 'Spirit of Ecstasy' instantly identifies the product **ILLUSTRATION 67**. An extremely unusual campaign for Rolls-Royce started in 1954 and comprised almost abstract photographs using reflections and distortions created by the bodywork. Only the 'Spirit of Ecstasy' emblem and the familiar slogan identify the product **ILLUSTRATION 68**. A classic advertisement for Rolls-Royce by David Ogilvy in the mid-1950s drew attention to the car's smooth and quiet engine: 'At 60 miles an hour the loudest noise in this new Rolls-Royce comes from the electric clock'.

ILLUSTRATION 69

1958

Meanwhile, in America towards the end of the decade, cars were getting longer and wider. An advertisement for Ford in 1958 shows the huge range of models produced by the company – all of them with the long, wide look of the Fifties **ILLUSTRATION 69**. An advertisement for Oldsmobile in 1951 continues the military and space-age imagery and the car itself was fitted with a missile-like feature on the hood **ILLUSTRATION 70**. The futuristic theme is repeated in an advertisement for Pontiac dated 1957 in which a monorail train is featured to represent the 'bold new generation' **ILLUSTRATION 71**. These exaggerated vehicles represented the feeling of optimism and invincibility in the United States.

Competition between manufacturers also became more and more fierce – more chrome, higher fins, longer bodies, more gadgets. Companies introduced new, often superfluous, features to tempt the customer and bump

ILLUSTRATION 70

National Geographic, 1951

ILLUSTRATION 71

Saturday Evening Post, 1958

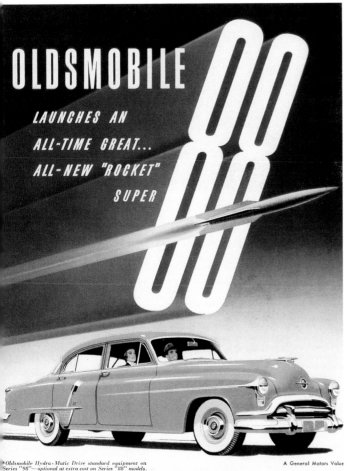

Oldsmobile Hydra-Matic Drive standard equipment on Series "98"—optional at extra cost on Series "88" models.

A General Motors Value

Brand new gas-saving "Rocket" Engine! Leader in high compression! Brilliant new Body by Fisher... bigger, wider, smarter, too! Luxurious new styling inside and out! More beauty—comfort—room and view! Completely new chassis—even smoother "Rocket" ride! A great new advancement in Hydra-Matic Drive*! See the triumphant new "Rocket 88"—and the glamorous new "Rocket 98"—at your Oldsmobile dealer's.

SEE THE SCENERY THROUGH THE ROOF—see traffic lights easily—yet tinted transparent top protects against heat, wind, glare.

Presenting The Sun Valley—
America's First Transparent-Top Car

You've seen pictures of dream cars of tomorrow. But you couldn't drive them, couldn't buy them. Now—for 1954—Mercury presents America's first transparent top car to be put into regular production.

There's a new, entirely different feeling in driving the Sun Valley. The entire front half of the roof is Plexiglas, tinted to ward off the heat and glare of the sun. You have a wonderful sensation of driving with no top at all—except that you enjoy the wind and weather protection of a standard sedan or hardtop.

But the Sun Valley is far more than the forerunner of a new style trend. Like all other 1954 Mercurys, it's powered by the new 161-horsepower Mercury V-8 engine that makes any driving easy. The new Mercury Sun Valley is bound to cause more comment and more excitement than anything else on the road for 1954. See it today at your Mercury dealer's!

MERCURY DIVISION · FORD MOTOR COMPANY

NEW 1954
MERCURY
A new kind of power
that makes _any_ driving easy

ILLUSTRATION 73

1958

ILLUSTRATION 74

1958

COOL...THINK I'LL SPEND THE SUMMER IN HERE!"

Enjoy a cool retreat from the heat. Just enter a Harrison Air Conditioned car—and step from simmering summer streets into a haven of cool, draft-free currents of clean, dehumidified air to every corner of your car. And with windows up you lock out wind, dirt and road noise. You'll emerge after every trip as clean, refreshed and neat as when you started.

Harrison's Custom "under the hood" Air Conditioning is designed for *all* 1958 General Motors cars. Also available now . . . the thrifty "under the dash" *Cool-Pack* for the new Chevrolet, Pontiac and Buick.* So, whether you're already driving your '58 or just about to buy, ask your GM dealer today about Harrison Air Conditioning.
Also available on most 1958 Chevrolet trucks.

cool air by the carload

HARRISON
AUTOMOTIVE AIR CONDITIONING

A GM PRODUCT—AVAILABLE AT
YOUR GENERAL MOTORS DEALER

ON RADIATOR DIVISION, GENERAL MOTORS CORPORATION, LOCKPORT, N.Y.

MIDSEASON SENSATION...NEW WINDSOR DARTLINE

It's all Chrysler and you'll like the price!

You want to just stand back and drink in this brilliant new Chrysler with its glistening new chromework and sparkling new colors.

But the real excitement comes when you get in and get going. The moment your hands touch the wheel you sense that this car wasn't made to sit still. You touch a button and in seconds you're effortlessly out on the open road.

As it irons out the rough spots, you know why Chrysler pioneered Torsion-Aire Ride. Under your foot you feel a reservoir of power, thanks to Chrysler's TorqueFlite transmission.

The stopping power of its sure-footed Total-Contact Brakes is more than a match for Chrysler's incredible go power. Styled for attraction, engineered for action—this Chrysler is *all* car. It's a car you drive because you want to, not just because you have to.

And it's never been so easy to step up to Chrysler. You can own the magnificent new Chrysler *Windsor Dartline* for only a few dollars a month more than most small cars!

See it—price it—at your Chrysler dealer today. Chrysler's a thrill you shouldn't miss.

EXTRA!

AMAZING NEW

auto-pilot

A Chrysler Engineering Exclusive that patrols your speed . . . conserves gas . . . lets you cruise accelerator-free.

SEE AND DRIVE **THE MIGHTY CHRYSLER DARTLINE**

up prices. In 1954, Ford introduced the first transparent roof in the Mercury **ILLUSTRATION 72** and General Motors used a rather unfriendly image of an aggressive polar bear to advertise its air-conditioning option

ILLUSTRATION 73. An advertisement for the Chrysler Dartline from 1958 promoted a cruise option brand-named 'auto-pilot' – another aircraft reference **ILLUSTRATION 74**. The 1959 Cadillac was probably the

ILLUSTRATION 75

Saturday Evening Post, 1958

epitome of the American 'dream car' with its huge tail fins and missile-like structure symbolising American superiority **ILLUSTRATION 75**.

Nevertheless, with the successful launch of the Soviet space craft, Sputnik, the bubble of confidence was burst and the slide into recession began. 1958 was the worst year in America for car sales since the end of the war. Sputnik shattered the myth of America's technological and military superiority and many newspapers chided Americans for being more concerned with comfort and consumerism than the defence of the nation. In *Life* magazine, the editor wrote, 'we should each decide what we really want most in the world… a Cadillac? A color

television? Or to live in freedom?' (*Life* magazine, 18 November 1957, pp.126–8). By the end of the decade the ostentation of the dream car, dubbed 'jukebox on wheels' by designer Raymond Loewy, was in decline. The popularity of smaller European cars was on the increase especially among the wealthy looking for distinction and individuality. By 1959, 10 per cent of the American automobile market comprised European cars. An advertisement for Plymouth from 1959 reflects this shift in consciousness from the ostentatious display of power and wealth, to slightly guilty restraint and humility. It seems that the garish extremes of the obsession with the American dream car may have been overindulgent after all **ILLUSTRATION 76**.

ILLUSTRATION 76

Saturday Evening Post, 1959

GOOD TASTE IS NEVER EXTREME

tain people have it. Certain things, as well—that sense of right-
s we call good taste. You recognize it at once when it is there.

It is there in the '59 Plymouth, in the look, the lines of a car
berately designed with flair, and with restraint. For good taste is

neither stodgy nor bizarre. It is not conspicuous. Nor is it anony-
mous. It does stand out, yes—but handsomely.

This year, so many people of good taste are responding to the
car fashioned most particularly for them—the '59 Plymouth.

today's best buy, tomorrow's best trade

Chapter 6

Think small

I f the 1950s was the golden age of American cars, the 1960s saw a more cautious and varied approach to selling cars. In America, the automobile was still the primary symbol of status and aspiration, but the beginning of the decade saw the stirrings of a creative revolution in advertising technique. Advertisers were discovering that in order to attract the attention of the customer and to impart their messages, they would need to challenge and amuse.

In Britain, the car was becoming a more universal acquisition and consumers would not ask themselves 'do we need a car?', but 'which car shall we buy?' In 1960s Britain, one in ten people owned a car, but by 1970 this figure had almost doubled (Stevenson, 2005, p.ix). Advertising themes of the period, particularly in Britain, were youth, vigour, style, affluence and the driving opportunities offered by the extensive motorway and road building programmes.

Surprisingly, car producers in Britain did not take advantage of the new opportunities of television advertising which began in 1955. The leading companies, Ford, Vauxhall, Chrysler and British Leyland, signed a secret agreement not to venture into the world of television advertising. They feared the rising costs and associated risks of committing to these expensive and untested methods. This cartel was finally broken in the 1970s when Datsun started a major television advertising campaign. The original agreement meant that printed

Why do Riley owners look so dashed superior?

Test-drive the new twin-carb. Riley Kestrel—and you'll find out

RILEY KESTREL
for magnificent motoring

The BRITISH Motor Corporation Ltd.
Backed by BMC Service—Express, Expert, Everywhere
Riley Motors Ltd., Sales Division, Longbridge, Birmingham
Overseas Division: BMC Export Sales Ltd., Birmingham
& 44/46 Piccadilly, London W.1.

See why the Kestrel's the world's most compact, most luxurious sporting five-seater. Note the real-leather luxury, the rich gleam of natural wood, the door-to-door welcome of deep-pile carpets. Here's space and comfort that only an east-west engine and Hydrolastic ® suspension can give you. Here's twin-carburetter performance and disc-brake safety and the kind of road-holding you get only with front-wheel drive.

Are you the sporty Kestrel type? Would you care to join the club? Then see your Riley dealer. The Kestrel is £780 18s. 9d., including £135 18s. 9d. P.T. The test-drive is free. And the footman can be hired.

ILLUSTRATION 77

The Illustrated London News, 1965

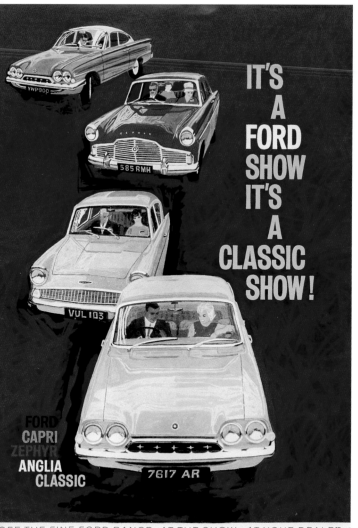

IT'S A FORD SHOW IT'S A CLASSIC SHOW!

FORD
CAPRI
ZEPHYR
ANGLIA
CLASSIC

SEE THE FINE FORD RANGE—AT THE SHOW · AT YOUR DEALER

advertising remained the most important way of persuading the public to buy new cars.

Colour photography was being used more commonly in advertisements. Generally, photography had been used in car advertising for the more affordable cars and more stylish, atmospheric illustrations were used for luxury cars. However, this simplistic division became blurred in the 1960s as more sophisticated photographic techniques were being used. An advertisement for the Riley Kestrel from 1965 is a typical example of the straightforward message offered by the conventional side-on photograph ILLUSTRATION 77. An advertisement for the Ford Show in 1961 shows how stylised illustrative techniques can offer a more vibrant image ILLUSTRATION 78. Two other examples show how developments in photographic skills shifted the way photographs were used in car advertisements. In 1963, Jaguar played on its slogan 'A different breed of cat', with an image of the car as a predatory animal stalking its prey ILLUSTRATION 79. MG used an excitingly animate photograph of its car which cleverly gave the impression of motion and speed ILLUSTRATION 80.

ILLUSTRATION 79

1963

A different breed of cat.
The 1964 Jaguar XK-E Coupe. $5,525 (P.O.E.) fully equipped.

When you get a sudden irresistible urge to go nowhere in particular ... clock up the miles ... feel the whip of the wind. Is it love, fate — or a slight touch of the compulsive, highly contagious MGB's? Is yours a restless, driving, nagging, aching, yearning, longing to proceed immediately to your nearest MG showroom? Why fight it? Remember: MGB drivers never travel alone. MGB £855.5.0 (including £148.15.0 PT)

ILLUSTRATION 80

Veteran and Vintage Magazine, 1967

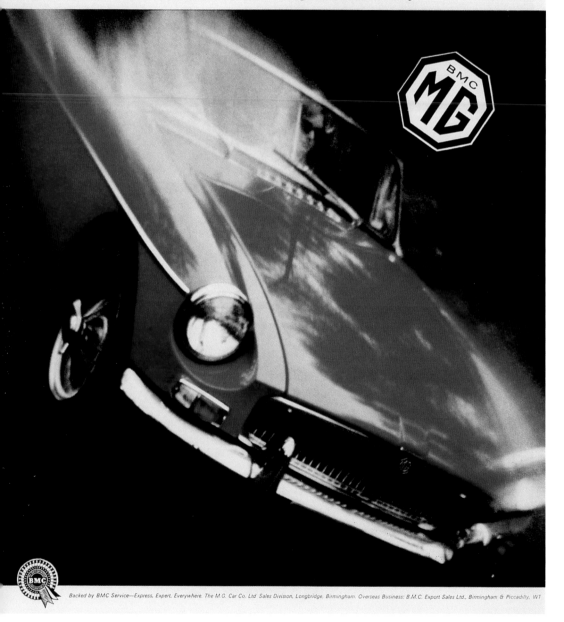

Backed by BMC Service—Express, Expert, Everywhere. The M.G. Car Co. Ltd Sales Division, Longbridge, Birmingham. Overseas Business: B.M.C. Export Sales Ltd., Birmingham & Piccadilly, W1

IVE INTO THE MOTORWAY AGE!

See them at your Vauxhall dealer's, and have a trial run.

The motorway age is for Vauxhalls! New '61 Vauxhalls. For instance, the Victor shown here. What's new in this fine four-cylinder car? *A lot's new!* New crisp styling and colour schemes. New grille at front. Vast new window at rear. New instrument panel and (in de Luxe model) padded facia. Then there are all sorts of technical things that you, Madam, are supposed not to bother about. But why not tell your husband? Mention new big-end bearings for long, long engine life at motorway speeds. Mention the all-synchro gearbox (you'll adore this yourself, it makes driving so easy!), and superb road holding and powerful brakes, and underbody sealing . . . Take him by the hand to your nearest Vauxhall-dealer and have a free outing together in the new Victor.

VICTOR £510 + £213.12.6 PT (£723.12.6)
VICTOR SUPER £535 + £224.0.10 PT (£759.0.10)
VICTOR DE LUXE £565 + £236.10.10 PT (£801.10.10)
VICTOR ESTATE CAR £605 + £253.4.2 PT (£858.4.2)
CRESTA 6-cylinder £715 + £299.0.10 PT (£1,014.0.10)
VELOX 6-cylinder £655 + £274.0.10 PT (£929.0.10)
On both Crestas and Velox, Hydra-matic transmission or overdrive are optional at extra cost

Vauxhall Motors Limited · Luton · Bedfordshire

EVERYONE DRIVES BETTER IN A VAUXHALL

ILLUSTRATION 81

1960

In the hopping, shopping, bargain grabbing bustle of the High Street you'll be glad you chose a Wolseley Hornet—effortless to drive, economical to run and easy to park.

WOLSELEY HORNET Mk III. *Prices from:*—
£628.11.11 (including £118.11.11 p.t.)

BMC WOLSELEY
BACKED BY BMC SERVICE—
Express, Expert, Everywhere
THE BRITISH MOTOR CORPORATION LTD

NOW with wind-away front windows, new ventilation system, concealed door hinges, push-button door handles and remote control gear lever. A noteworthy feature is the larger than Mini engine: 998 c.c.

WOLSELEY MOTORS LIMITED (SALES DIVISION) LONGBRIDGE, BIRMINGHAM · Overseas Business: BMC Export Sales Limited, Birmingham. Personal Exports Division: 41-46 Piccadilly, London W 1

ILLUSTRATION 82

The Illustrated London News, 1967

Many 1960s car advertisements reflect the changes in culture and the economy during that decade. The first motorway, the M6 Preston By-pass, was opened in 1958 and most of the M1 in 1959. An advertisement for Vauxhall in 1960 reflected the optimism for the new 'motorway age' ILLUSTRATION 81. A lovely advertisement for Wolseley from 1967 incorporated signs and symbols of the developments in consumerism, such as 'self-service', 'delicatessen' and the wire shopping basket

ILLUSTRATION 82. In 1966, the food manufacturers Heinz had a competition to promote its products and the prizes were fifty-seven (of course) specially converted Wolseley Hornets. Crayford Engineering of Westerham in Kent was commissioned to create these unique convertibles and the winners received numerous extras such as a picnic case, an electric kettle (to fit the electric point in the boot) and a tartan rug! Forty-two of these original cars are still in existence.

ILLUSTRATION 83

Esquire, 1962

This beauty eats mountains for breakfast—Pontiac Grand Prix! Point the G.P. uphill, and you find its 303 h.p. Trophy V-8 flattens towering grades almost casually. (And by paying a bit more, you can pick from engines ranging way on up in horsepower.) The custom-styled G.P. doesn't just look like a finely honed piece of road machinery—it is, in fact, the real article. Let's tick off some of the reasons: Deep-cradling bucket seats, center console with tach, plus floor-mounted Hydra-Matic and four-speed stick as extra-cost options. And the G.P., you'll be happy to know, has Pontiac's road-wedded Wide-Track. See your Pontiac dealer—the G.P. man. Pontiac Motor Division, General Motors Corporation.

Grand Prix

In Britain and America, foreign travel was becoming more affordable too and many car advertisements reflected this new interest in continental touring. An advertisement for Pontiac in 1962 incorporated an exotic illustration of the south of France, and in Britain in 1961 the Rover Company used images of various overseas locations in an almost cinematic way **ILLUSTRATIONS 83 and 84**. The Rover P5, as illustrated in this advertisement, was a hugely successful car favoured by government officials and the Queen. It was launched in 1958 and a succession of British prime ministers used it as their official car: Harold Wilson, Ted Heath, Jim Callaghan and Margaret Thatcher. Harold Wilson had a special pipe holder fitted in his official P5. A new, more powerful model with a V8 engine was introduced in 1967, ironically in time for the Government's introduction of the 70mph speed limit.

ILLUSTRATION 84

Punch, 1961

Punch, May 24 1961

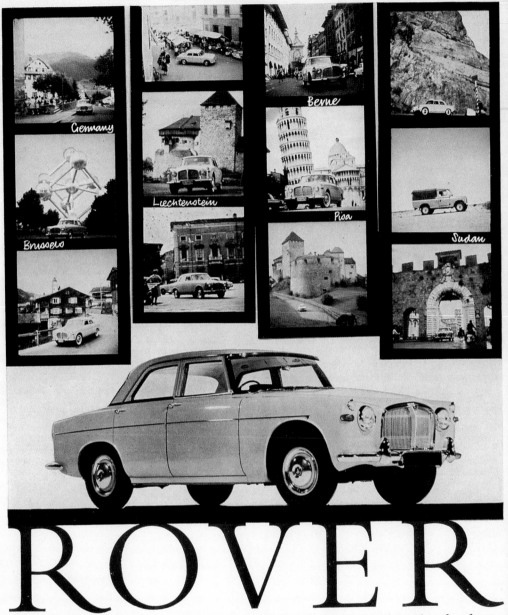

It was born and bred to cross the frontiers of the world, this Rover 3-Litre. It combines the grace and comfort of a town carriage with the dash—and stamina—necessary for long distance motoring. On the 3-Litre power steering is an optional extra. On all three Rover models—the 80, 100 and 3-Litre—front wheel disc brakes and overdrive are standard equipment.

The '80', £1,396.10.10d. The '100', £1,538.4.2d. The '3-Litre' with conventional gearbox, £1,783.5.10d., with automatic transmission £1,864.0.10d. (Prices include P.T.)

THE ROVER COMPANY LIMITED, SOLIHULL, WARWICKSHIRE. *Makers of fine cars and the world famous Land-Rover.*

¡Viva Anglia!

Viva the **excitement** of driving the Anglia—hugging the tightest bends, gliding down the motorway with sports car verve. Viva the **comfort** of the Anglia—the 4-seat roominess, the saloon-car reliability. Viva the **economy** of driving the Anglia—up to 50 mpg and low running costs backed by Ford Service. Viva Anglia—the world's most exciting light car!

EVERY NATION HAS ITS GREAT CAR—BRITAIN'S IS THE **ANGLIA**!

FORD OF BRITAIN *Ford*

ILLUSTRATION 85

1962

Meet **ANGLIA**. Shopping is more fun when you let ANGL that staunch Briton, carry the load! The big trunk helps. So does ANGL supersmooth handling. Sports-type 4-speed transmission. More leg-re head-room, too. Bigger doors for regal entrances. More glass all arou and note that zippy Z-line rear window! Best of all, economy: superbly b ANGLIA costs about $1600* with full dashboard instrumentation. Gets u 40 m.p.g. which means it can save (counting everything) up to 9¢ per n Going shopping in town? ANGLIA savings will treat you to lunch!

Get the **LION**'s share of driving fun!

LOOK FOR THIS SIGN. *English FORD Line* CHOOSE FROM 12 MODELS IN THE ENGLISH FORD LINE, INCL ANGLIA, PREFECT, CONSUL, ZEPHYR, ZODIAC, AND THAMES VANS. FOR THE NAME OF YOUR NE DEALER, CALL YOUR LOCAL WESTERN UNION OPERATOR 25.

Made in England for the Ford Motor Company, Dearborn, Mich. Sold and serviced in the United States by selected dealers. For further information write Imported Car Sales, Ford M 3000 Schaefer Rd., Dearborn, Mich. *Mfr.'s. suggested retail price at Eastern & Gulf ports of entry. State and local taxes and transportation from POE extra. Price subject to change

ILLUSTRATION 86

1960

The car was gradually phased out as a ministerial car in the 1980s during Thatcher's term of office and was replaced by the Jaguar XJ which continued to transport prime ministers into the 2000s.

Following the oil embargo resulting from the Suez Crisis in 1956, car manufacturers were putting their efforts into the design and production of smaller, more economical cars. Petrol rationing was reintroduced in Britain and while car sales generally plummeted, the sales of so-called 'bubble cars', mainly produced in Germany, soared. British manufacturers worked to cash in on this market. Distinctive small British cars of the 1960s included the Ford Anglia 105E. The reversed rear-window was inspired by the Fiat 600 produced in 1955 and the prominent eye-like headlamps and tail fins were influenced by American designs. Production of this model continued until 1967 **ILLUSTRATIONS 85 and 86**. The Ford Anglia was introduced

Wizardry on wheels!

"QUALITY FIRST"
MORRIS *MINI-MINOR*

Never before has such quality, performance, economy and sheer reliability been offered to so many—at so low a price!

The Morris Mini-Minor carries four big adults and as much luggage as they're ever likely to need. It has a full-size 4-cylinder engine of proven design which leaves you with 10 m.p.h. in hand even when cruising at 60! Its fuel economy of up to 50 m.p.g. means pounds in your pocket at the end of each quarter.

It's easy to see how much extra space is achieved by the brilliant 'East-West' engine. But that's only the first touch of genius.

Gearbox, transmission, steering, are all incorporated in one amazingly simple power pack unit.

There's four wheel independent suspension for a smooth ride over the roughest roads. There's front wheel drive for wonderfully accurate, finger-tip control.

The Morris Mini-Minor is ten years ahead of its time.

★ Revolutionary engine mounted "East-West" across the frame!

★ Revolutionary "power pack" engine unit contains steering, gearbox and differential!

★ Revolutionary performance! 70 m.p.h. and up to 50 m.p.g. from an 850 c.c. engine!

★ Revolutionary space—planned interior for full family comfort!

★ Revolutionary luggage capacity—storage space wherever you look!

★ Revolutionary 4 wheel independent suspension makes all roads seem smooth!

12 MONTHS' WARRANTY and backed by B.M.C. Service—the most comprehensive in Europe.

World's most exciting car...with engine mounted

EAST WEST

across the frame

IT'S WIZARDRY ON WHEELS AND 'QUALITY FIRST' ALL THROUGH

£350 Plus £146.19.2 Purchase Tax
DE LUXE MODEL £378.10 Plus £158.16.8 Purchase Tax

MORRIS MOTORS LTD., COWLEY, OXFORD. LONDON DISTRIBUTORS: MORRIS HOUSE, BERKELEY SQ., W.I. OVERSEAS BUSINESS: NUFFIELD EXPORTS LTD., OXFORD AND AT 41-46 PICCADILLY, LONDON, W.I

ILLUSTRATION 87

The Illustrated London News, 1959

in the same year, and was roughly the same price as the Austin Se7en (Morris Mini Minor) which was to become an icon of 1960s design. The Morris engineer Alec Issigonis designed the Mini, which was only ten-feet long, with 80 per cent of the length accommodating passengers and the remaining 20 per cent for the engine and luggage. The engine was turned sideways and the gearbox was put in the sump **ILLUSTRATION 87**. Issigonis had the idea that an uncomfortable driver would be more alert and devised a contorted driving position on safety grounds.

ILLUSTRATION 88

The Tatler and Bystander, 1964

NEW
CORTINA
SUPER

Extra power! Extra luxury!

Ford extend the Cortina range—and add to the Cortina standard and
De Luxe models a new sparkling Cortina Super, with 5-bearing crankshaft
1500cc engine (now optional on standard and De Luxe models) and luxury
interior fittings. Outside too there's a new distinguished big-car look. Get
the feel of this Super Cortina yourself. Your Ford dealer will gladly arrange
a no-obligation test drive.

5-bearing crankshaft 1500cc engine giving 0-60 take off in 19.5 secs. Top speed into the 80's. Yet up
to 35 mpg. 4-speed all-synchro box. Luxury fittings. Generous 5-seater roominess. Glide-Ride suspension.
Every 5,000 miles or twice a year service. 12 months/12,000 miles warranty. Low-cost fixed-price Ford
Service. Attractive hp/insurance rates.

FROM ONLY **£669**·19·7 TAX PAID

4-door model (illustrated) from only £688.2.1 (tax paid)

MADE WITH CARE BY
FORD OF BRITAIN

ILLUSTRATION 89

The New Yorker, 1962

Think small.

Our little car isn't so much of a novelty
any more.

A couple of dozen college kids don't
try to squeeze inside it.

The guy at the gas station doesn't ask
where the gas goes.

Nobody even stares at our shape.

In fact, some people who drive our little

flivver don't even think 32 miles to the gallon is going any great guns.

Or using five pints of oil instead of five
quarts.

Or never needing anti-freeze.

Or racking up 40,000 miles on a set of
tires.

That's because once you get used to

some of our economies, you don't ev
think about them any more.

Except when you squeeze into a sm
parking spot. Or renew your small in
ance. Or pay a small repair
Or trade in your old VW fo
new one.

Think it over.

The Ford Cortina, a mid-sized family car which became a best-seller, was introduced in 1962. It is rumoured that the original name given to this model was 'Caprino', but when it was discovered that the word meant 'goat dung' in Italian, the name of the stylish alpine venue of the 1956 Winter Olympics, Cortina d'Ampezzo, was chosen instead ILLUSTRATION 88.

In America, there was also a growing interest in small cars and particularly in foreign cars. The most successful of these was the Volkswagen Beetle. The original 'people's car' was designed by the Porsche company in the 1930s with backing from Hitler, and a handful were produced before the start of the war. However, mass-production did not start until 1948. The Beetle became the top-selling foreign car in the United States and globally sold over twenty million by the 1990s. Its American success was partly due to the revolutionary advertising campaign created by Bill Bernbach, the founder of New York advertising agency Doyle Dane Bernbach. Many consider this campaign to have ushered in the era of modern advertising, a 'creative revolution' by using techniques that challenged, surprised and engaged the viewer. The first in the series Bernbach produced for Volkswagen was the 'Think Small' advertisement in 1960 ILLUSTRATION 89. His subsequent advertisements for the Beetle paved the way for honest and self-effacing advertising that addressed the viewer with respect and intelligence. Bernbach summed up his philosophy: 'I wouldn't hesitate for a second to choose the plain looking ad that is alive and

ILLUSTRATION 90

1962

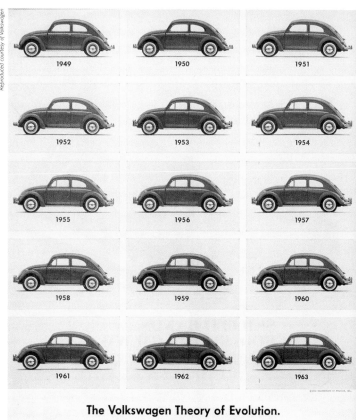

The Volkswagen Theory of Evolution.

ILLUSTRATION 91

The New Yorker, 1965

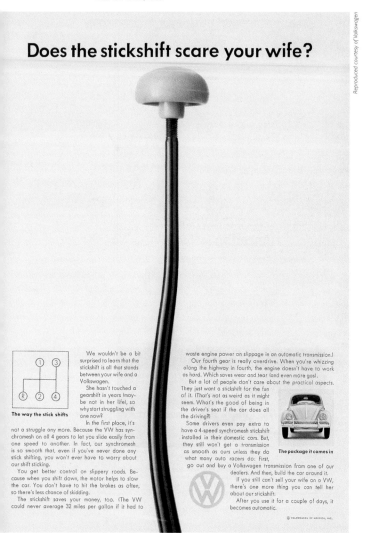

Reproduced courtesy of Volkswagen

Does the stickshift scare your wife?

The way the stick shifts

We wouldn't be a bit surprised to learn that the stickshift is all that stands between your wife and a Volkswagen.

She hasn't touched a gearshift in years (maybe not in her life), so why start struggling with one now?

In the first place, it's not a struggle any more. Because the VW has synchromesh on all 4 gears to let you slide easily from one speed to another. In fact, our synchromesh is so smooth that, even if you've never done any stick shifting, you won't ever have to worry about our shift sticking.

You get better control on slippery roads. Because when you shift down, the motor helps to slow the car. You don't have to hit the brakes as often, so there's less chance of skidding.

The stickshift saves your money, too. (The VW could never average 32 miles per gallon if it had to

waste engine power on slippage in an automatic transmission.)

Our fourth gear is really overdrive. When you're whizzing along the highway in fourth, the engine doesn't have to work as hard. Which saves wear and tear (and even more gas).

But a lot of people don't care about the practical aspects. They just want a stickshift for the fun of it. (That's not as weird as it might seem. What's the good of being in the driver's seat if the car does all the driving?)

Some drivers even pay extra to have a 4-speed synchromesh stickshift installed in their domestic cars. But, they still won't get a transmission as smooth as ours unless they do

The package it comes in

what many auto racers do: First, go out and buy a Volkswagen transmission from one of our dealers. And then, build the car around it.

If you still can't sell your wife on a VW, there's one more thing you can tell her about our stickshift:

After you use it for a couple of days, it becomes automatic.

© VOLKSWAGEN OF AMERICA, INC.

---

vital and meaningful, over the ad that is beautiful but dumb' (Saunders, 1999, p.191). Another in the series showed images of the Volkswagen from 1949 to 1963 that presented it as little altered, and mocked the traditional car industry policy of inbuilt obsolescence and annual model 'improvements' **ILLUSTRATION 90**.

A rather sexist example of Bernbach's VW advertisements in 1965, which seems to imply that women are intimidated by the difficulty of driving a manual car, illustrates how the immediately recognisable campaign uses simple black-and-white photographic images and an unusual amount of white space. The ambiguous tag-line challenges the viewer to work out the slightly obscure meaning **ILLUSTRATION 91**.

British advertisers picked up on this new approach. An advertisement for the new Rover in 1969 cleverly incorporates an eye-catching image of a yellow balloon and an ambiguous tag-line that makes the viewer look again to try to establish its meaning. This advertisement also indicates the slow shift in safety awareness that began to take place in the second half of the 1960s **ILLUSTRATION 92**.

ILLUSTRATION 92

The Illustrated London News, 1969

Car manufacturers had generally tended to avoid mentioning safety features in their products, assuming that their customers would not want to be reminded of the dangers of driving. Ralph Nader's 1965 book, *Unsafe at Any Speed*, accused car makers of being obsessed with styling and profit rather than building safe, economical cars. Subsequent national debates led to the National Traffic and Motor Vehicle Safety Act in 1966 in America, and safety-consciousness began to be a more significant issue in automobile marketing.

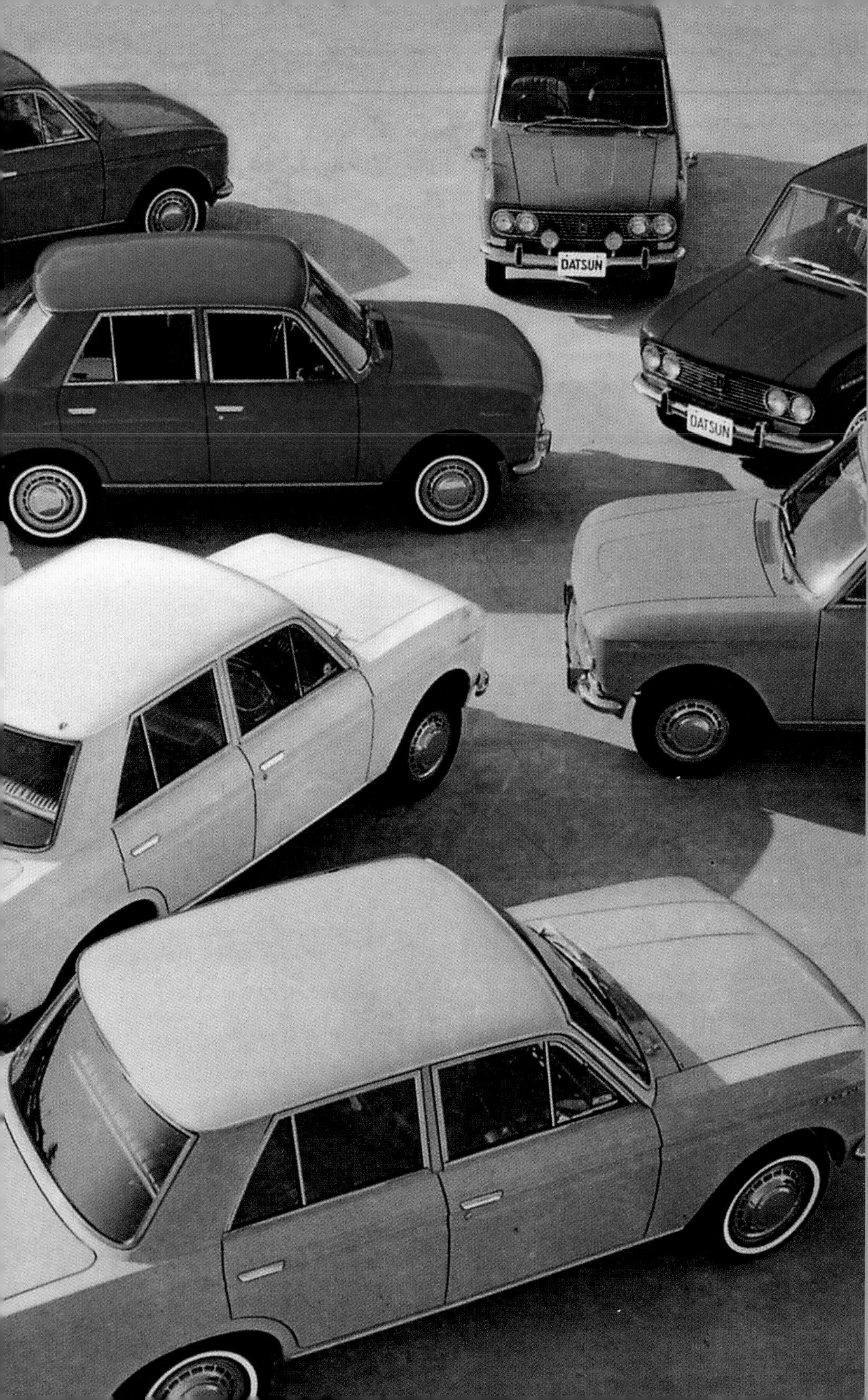

Chapter 7

1970s

Safety first

uge increases in traffic levels, the rise in oil prices and general awareness of environmental responsibility all led to a trend in automobile advertising during the 1970s towards safety, efficiency, cleaner emissions and a general reduction in car sizes.

The rise in traffic levels in Britain, particularly as a result of the motorway and road building programmes of the 1960s, included private motorists and, more significantly, lorries. Accident and road mortality rates were on the rise and some car manufacturers resisted the fear that by reminding drivers of the risks of motoring in their advertisements they might associate their products with danger. Volvo was (and still is) at the forefront in emphasising safety in its advertising campaigns. The Swedish company started to develop seat-belt technology in the 1950s and in 1959 was the first car manufacturer to introduce the three-point belt as standard in its new cars. Since then, Volvo has used the recurrent themes of safety, reliability and durability in its campaigns; themes that have been developed imaginatively and very successfully over the years. An advertisement for Volvo dated 1978 shows a mother driving away from a very privileged girls' school carrying several young girls as passengers. The image and text emphasise the protection that the car gives its precious contents, as well as using symbols of privilege and prestige **ILLUSTRATION 93**.

AT VOLVO WE DEMAND STRENGTH
FROM THE CAR, NOT THE DRIVER.

IT'S GETTING BETTER ALL THE TIME

ILLUSTRATION 93

1978

ILLUSTRATION 94

1973

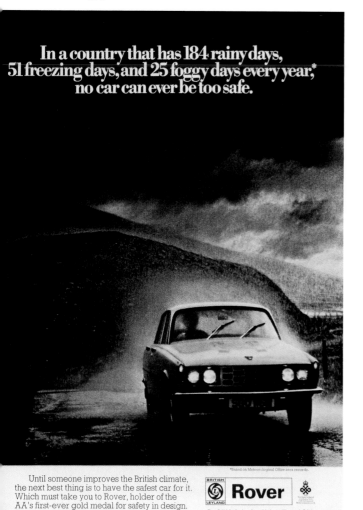

In a country that has 184 rainy days, 51 freezing days, and 25 foggy days every year,* no car can ever be too safe.

*Based on Meteorological Office area records.

Until someone improves the British climate, the next best thing is to have the safest car for it. Which must take you to Rover, holder of the AA's first-ever gold medal for safety in design.

Rover

From British Leyland – makers of the best-selling cars in Britain.

Another manufacturer that emphasised safety themes was Rover. The Rover P6 series was introduced in 1963 but produced well into the 1970s. When it was launched, it won several industry awards for safety innovations. An advertisement for the car in 1973 highlights the dangers and difficulties of driving in adverse weather conditions in Britain, but the copy reassures the reader by referring to the AA medal for safety in design, even though that had been awarded almost a decade earlier ILLUSTRATION 94.

At this time, most Americans did not wear seat belts. In 1974, the National Highway Traffic Safety Administration (NHTSA) instructed car manufacturers to install seat belt/ignition interlock devices in all new cars so that a car wouldn't start unless the front seat occupants were belted. This infringement of American concepts of individual freedom caused uproar and Congress forced the NHTSA to repeal the standard.

Before Ralph Nader's indictment of the motor industry's attitude to automobile safety, American consumers had seen small (generally imported) cars as unsafe. In the 1970s, Japanese cars had an improving reputation and the style and functionality of imported cars had growing appeal. The 1973 oil crisis triggered the growth in sales of Japanese cars because they were small and economical to run on increasingly expensive petrol. In that year, the Organisation of Petroleum Exporting Countries (OPEC) declared that it would no longer ship petroleum to nations who had supported Israel during the Yom Kippur

Busily talking...

are the DATSUN owners about motoring happiness.

ILLUSTRATION 95

1970s

War, primarily Britain and the United States. The restrictions led to high petrol prices, a series of recessions and high inflation. In America, the price of petrol rose from 38.5 cents in 1973 to just over 55 cents in 1974. Japanese cars had a reputation for being far more fuel efficient than the gas-guzzling American product. In the 1960s, Japanese car manufacturers had specialised in producing small, cheap 'kei cars' with small engines for the domestic market. When petrol prices rose, these smaller cars became more attractive to consumers in the West. An advertisement for Datsun from the early 1970s shows examples of the range of compact, functional and economical Japanese cars that were to be so popular ILLUSTRATION 95.

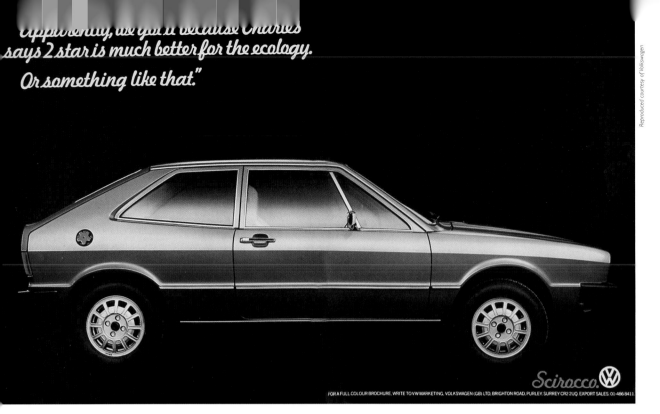

apparently, we got it because Charles says 2 star is much better for the ecology. Or something like that."

Scirocco. VW

FOR A FULL COLOUR BROCHURE, WRITE TO VW MARKETING, VOLKSWAGEN (GB) LTD, BRIGHTON ROAD, PURLEY, SURREY CR2 2UQ. EXPORT SALES: 01-486 8411.

ILLUSTRATION 97

Telegraph Sunday Magazine, 1977

ILLUSTRATION 96

Country Life, 1973

How to copy today's Land-Rover

1. Allow 25 years for research and development. 2. Build 750,000 examples. Test in 140 overseas territories, on every exercise from famine relief and mountain rescue to frontier patrolling and glider-launching. 3. Find network of 700 dealers with 25 years' knowledge of vehicle. Keep spares cheap and abundant. 4. Make servicing easy, and infrequent. 5. Produce 15,000 variants of vehicle.

Arrange for specialist makers to produce complete range of auxiliary equipment from sewage-pumps to snow ploughs. 6. Try to equal Land-Rover re-sale value. 7. Try to shake stubborn conviction of Land-Rover owners that they've got a virtually indestructible and infinitely versatile vehicle, and anything else is a poor imitation, and poor value for money in the long run.

BRITISH LEYLAND — Land-Rover

There's no substitute for the versatile Land-Rover.

The Japanese had a reputation in the West for copying successful products and reproducing them more economically. An advertisement for Land-Rover in 1973, illustrates the prejudices and fears of British industry that 'foreign' companies will steal their ideas and undercut their prices **ILLUSTRATION 96**.

In addition to economic reasons for the shift to more fuel-efficient cars, there were the origins of the environmental movement in the 1970s. Interest in this field centred mainly on anti-nuclear protests and the protection of animals in danger of extinction, but there was growing awareness too of the impact of exhaust emissions on the environment. An advertisement for the VW Scirocco in 1977 is an example of this growing awareness and also hints that if you don't know about

ILLUSTRATION 98

Punch, 1976

Sex has never been a problem for us.

6 out of every 10 British Minis® on the road are probably being driven by women.

With current attitudes towards sex discrimination, we have to be careful how we explain that fact.

Perhaps we shouldn't say women like Minis because they're happy, exciting cars to drive. Or that they appeal to the female money-sense by being so astoundingly economical. Or that women are crazy about a Mini's undeniable ability to stay stylish and fashionable. Or that Supercover after-sales protection takes a load off a woman's mind. Or that the new comfort and luxury of the Mini pampers the gentle sex.

If we said any of those things, we might be accused of discriminating in favour of women.

So it's probably better if we just carry on making marvellous Minis for discriminating...er...people. OK?

Mini

From Leyland Cars. With Supercover.

®'Mini' is a Registered Trade Mark.

'the ecology', you really should ILLUSTRATION 97. Incidentally, '2-star' petrol, mentioned in the advertisement, was a low-octane fuel and was gradually replaced by unleaded petrol in the 1990s.

Despite the progress and achievements of the women's liberation movement in the 1970s, the text of the Scirocco advertisement makes the suggestion that women have a limited understanding of important issues. An advertisement for the ever-popular Mini in 1976 also makes patronising reference to the campaigns for awareness of sexual discrimination ILLUSTRATION 98. The copy immediately attracts attention with a daring double-meaning, 'Sex has never been a problem for us'. Then it

ILLUSTRATION 99
1979

It pulls beautifully.

The Triumph Spitfire's twin-carbed 1493cc engine gives you all the thrust you'd expect from a classic sportscar.
Yet, unlike other sportscars, it has a boot big enough for more than just your own suitcase. It can do over 50mpg.* And it costs less than £3,400.**
So go to your showroom for a test drive today and see what a great deal you'll get.

SPITFIRE

TRIUMPH

*OFFICIALLY CERTIFIED FUEL CONSUMPTION FIGURES SPITFIRE SIMULATED URBAN DRIVING 29.4 MPG (9.6 L/100 KM) AT 56 MPH (90 KPH) 50.2 MPG (5.6 L/100 KM), AT 75 MPH (120 KPH) 32.7 MPG (8.7 L/100 KM) THE FIGURES FOR YOUR CAR MAY DIFFER. ▪ Jaguar Rover Triumph Ltd.
** TRIUMPH SPITFIRE FROM £3385 (INCLUDES FRONT SEAT BELTS, CAR TAX AND VAT DELIVERY AND NUMBER PLATES EXTRA) PRICE CORRECT AT TIME OF GOING TO PRESS

goes on to refer to the care that must be taken to avoid being accused of discrimination 'with current attitudes towards sex discrimination, we have to be careful'. The copy then points out that it is trying to avoid discrimination in favour of women, 'perhaps we shouldn't say women like Minis because they're happy, exciting cars to drive', but the viewer would probably have been aware that the company was making a dig at the new Sex Discrimination Act of 1975. In a different and rather unsubtle 1979 advertisement for the Triumph Spitfire 1500, the tag-line, 'It pulls beautifully', refers to the large engine of this new model, but also reminds us of the enduring reason why male drivers would choose to buy a convertible sports car ILLUSTRATION 99.

Other advertisements also make reference to the more liberal lifestyle and sexual freedom of young people in the 1970s. A campaign for the MG Midget from 1973 included the tag-line 'Your mother wouldn't like it' ILLUSTRATION 100. A young couple have apparently spent a long night partying and have stopped at a workers' tea hut, the only place open in the early hours of the morning. The image of the MG Midget, built for fun, with its bright orange paint, pointed to the generation gap between the parents who had been through the war and the frivolous youth who just wanted to enjoy themselves.

One of the most successful and iconic cars of the 1970s was the Volkswagen Golf. Known as the 'Rabbit' in America, it replaced the streamlined Beetle that had been

ILLUSTRATION 100

1973

YOUR MOTHER WOULDN'T LIKE IT.

1275 cc. 94mph. 0-50 in 9·6 seconds.* £987·89†

† Including car tax and V.A.T. Number plates, seat belts and delivery charges extra. *Source Autocar

MG

From British Leyland
Makers of the best selling cars in Britain

MG MIDGET

The Rabbits
of Lahaska, Pennsylvania.

It's true.
Meet Peter Rabbit.
His wife, Bunny Rabbit.
Their son, Jay Rabbit.
And their brand-new Volkswagen Rabbit.

Now when we read about them in the newspaper, we couldn't wait to ask the big question:

"What was it that got you to add another Rabbit to the family?
The 38 miles to the gallon?"*

The incredible acceleration?
The handling ease?
The head and leg room inside of some mid-size cars?

The Hatchback, at no extra charge?
VW engineering? The low price?"

"It was all those things," answered Peter Rabbit.

"Plus something I've been fond of for 14 years," added Bunny.
"What's that?" we asked.
"My last name," she smiled.

rabbit VW

*38 mpg Highway—24 mpg City. Based on the 1975 Model Federal E.P.A. report.

ESQUIRE: JULY 21

ILLUSTRATION 101

Esquire, 1975

It flies through the air
with the greatest of ease

The aerodynamic Buick Regal.
When an object is shaped to reduce aerodynamic drag, it often becomes more handsome in the process. We think that fact is happily attested to by the two sleek profiles above, the one in the foreground being our Buick Regal.
With its low-sloping front end and high-sailing rear deck, Regal moves through the air easily, so it moves over the road efficiently. A factor which contributes to these rather gratifying mileage estimates.

30 EST. HWY. **21** EPA EST. MPG

And that, mind you, is for a Regal Limited Coupe, powered by a responsive 3.8 liter V-6. Fitted out with all our customary interior niceties and refinements.
Which shows you don't have to strip a car of comforts to achieve economy when you can outstrip the wind.
The aerodynamic Buick Regal. It flies through the air with the greatest of ease without even leaving the ground.
Use estimated MPG for comparison. Your mileage may differ depending on speed, distance, weather. Actual highway mileage lower. Estimates lower in California. Some Buicks are

equipped with engines pr other GM Divisions, subsid affiliated companies worle your Buick dealer for deta

BUIC

Wouldn't you really rather hav

ILLUSTRATION 102

1981

produced for about thirty years and was starting to decline in sales. The new car, despite being designed by the Italian car designer Giorgetto Giugiaro, had the look of German functionalism with its boxy design. The car inspired numerous copies and became Volkswagen's best-selling product. By 2007, over 25 million had been built. Giugiaro was voted the Car Designer of the Twentieth Century in 1999. A 1975 American advertisement for the Rabbit plays on the name of the

model and promotes its appeal as a family car, but also manages to list its numerous economic and practical features **ILLUSTRATION 101**.

Car advertising of the period reflected the economic turbulence and social changes of the 1970s, but there was still room for the celebration of technical achievement. An advertisement for Buick in 1981 uses the dramatic image of Concorde which had started flying commercially across

ILLUSTRATION 103

Country Life, 1972

It's taken motoring years ahead.

M62 Pennine Section by Sir Alfred McAlpine and Sons Ltd. Rover by British Leyland. ⑨ **Rover**

the Atlantic in 1976 ILLUSTRATION 102. The advertisement for Rover in 1972 shows a stretch of the M62 Pennine section, the building of which was a significant feat of engineering. This section of the motorway was completed in 1971 after overcoming extreme weather conditions and difficult terrain. Over nine million cubic meters of material had to be moved to build this road, including solid rock and peat bogs ILLUSTRATION 103.

Chapter 8

1980s

The ultimate
selling machine

ecause of the redirection of advertising budgets to television advertising, much of the printed advertising of the 1980s, particularly for the motor industry, was rather dull and unimaginative in comparison to other decades. Printed advertisements often supported and reinforced the messages pumped out from the television rather than relying on the static image to create its own impact. However, by the end of the decade, print advertising seemed to be gaining strength with the rise of specialist magazines, particularly those that served motor enthusiasts. Additionally, some agencies started to follow the lead of tobacco advertisers who were not allowed to advertise on television and had to work around stringent restrictions. It was noted that some of the challenging and inventive tobacco advertising campaigns in print could have dramatic impact and promotional success.

Many 1980s advertisements followed tried and tested paths. Rover, using the slogan 'success breeds success', appealed to the social aspirations of its customers, particularly playing on its reputation for providing cars for government ministers **ILLUSTRATION 104**. An advertisement for Range Rover in 1981 appealed to the snob who would like to have a double-barrelled surname **ILLUSTRATION 105**. An advertisement for the Volkswagen Jetta from 1980 uses an illustration which suggests the journey of the jet stream after which the car was named **ILLUSTRATION 106**. The Jetta was developed primarily for the American market. Volkswagen had noted that

Positions of Privilege.

Power can bring its own privileges.

Ask anyone who's experienced the ultimate Rover, the Vanden Plas. They'll tell you about the sheer pleasure of driving with the 155 bhp that flows from the superbly efficient V8 engine. About the luxury–and convenience–of cruise control. About thoughtful details, like the electrically operated steel sunroof and the remote-control electrically adjusted and demisted door mirrors.

Then talk to their passengers. They'll be more than happy to talk about the Connolly leather seats, the quiet comfort, the space, the balance-controlled 4-speaker stereo entertainment, the bronze-tinted electric windows. And much, much more.

The Vanden Plas heads the outstanding 5-car Rover range. Take any one of them for a test drive. Whichever Rover you choose, you're in for a privileged experience.

 **Rover**

2300/2300S/2600S/3500SE/VANDEN PLAS

Success breeds success.

ILLUSTRATION 104

Telegraph Sunday Magazine, 1981

There's only one car for the double-barrelled.

V8 engine, permanent four-wheel drive, power steering, and power-assisted braking. What other car on earth combines such power with such style?

RANGE ROVER
IT'S HOW THE SMOOTH TAKE THE ROUGH.

ILLUSTRATION 105

1981

Americans seemed to prefer more conventional sedans rather than Golf-like hatchbacks. Bentley also reverted to a very traditional look in its advertising. A 1984 advertisement for the Mulsanne-Turbo uses an illustration of similar style to advertisements of the 1930s **ILLUSTRATION 107**. This was a deliberate attempt to remind viewers of Bentley's long-standing reputation, while the copy emphasised the new power and technological developments such as the 'electronic knock sensor' (a device that can detect problems in engine timing).

Despite a prevalence of these more traditional advertising techniques in the 1980s, there were the stirrings of innovation in car advertising. In particular, BMW and Volvo started to lead the way in striking and innovative printed advertising. BMW (GB) was established in 1979 and the London-based advertising agency WCRS was appointed to develop its brand identity. WCRS developed a campaign based around the slogan, 'the ultimate driving machine' and used sophisticated photographic and lighting techniques to portray a product without a hint of fallibility. As Deyan

ILLUSTRATION 106

Telegraph Sunday Magazine, 1980

Volkswagen Jetta. Not another 4-door family saloon.

gen Jetta. 1300, 1500 and 1600cc. From £4,080. For a colour brochure contact Customer Enquiry Services, Volkswagen (GB) Ltd.   Yeomans Drive, Blakelands, Milton Keynes, MK14 5AN. (0908) 679121. Export Sales: 95 Baker Street, London W1M 1FB. 01-486 8411.

Sudjic, the editor of the design magazine *Blueprint*, has said, 'BMW is the first car company to treat us as grown ups… there is no such thing as a cheap BMW, there is no such thing as an ostentatious one… it doesn't have to raise its voice to gain respect.' (Stewart, 1995, p.15) The campaign was so successful that within fifteen years total sales for BMW had increased sixfold. A good example of one of WCRS's advertisements for BMW from 1982

ILLUSTRATION 107

The Illustrated London News, 1984

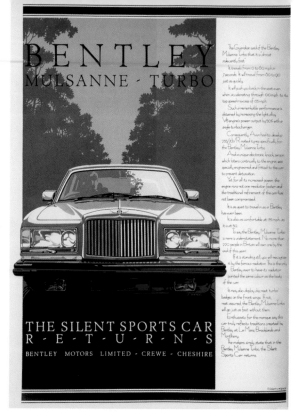

shows a dramatic image of a grey line of defunct cars arranged like gravestones in front of a dark, thunderous sky. The new BMW is presented as a victorious monarch having overcome all rivals. This is an excellent example of how more adventurous and ambitiously directed photographic images, almost in the mode of fashion photography, were being used for a wider range of consumer goods **ILLUSTRATION 108**.

ILLUSTRATION 108

Telegraph Sunday Magazine, 1982

ILLUSTRATION 109

The Illustrated London News, 1984

Another good example from the BMW campaign is the 'shaken… not stirred' advertisement from 1984 **ILLUSTRATION 109**. This image not only refers the viewer to the class, adventure and machismo of the famous James Bond phrase, but also conveys the quiet efficiency of the BMW engine. This theme continued for many years. A deceptively simple advertisement from 1988 compares the vibrations of its six-cylinder engine with more common four-cylinder engines. It not only imparts the primary message very effectively but, by using coloured magnetic letters that were very popular at the time as a learning tool for young children, makes a subliminal connection with responsible family protection and comfort **ILLUSTRATION 110**. This particular advertisement was published in *Vogue*, a magazine predominantly read by women. BMW initially monopolised a double-page colour spread advertisement in the Sunday newspaper colour supplements, to a point where readers came to expect a BMW advertisement as the first in the magazine.

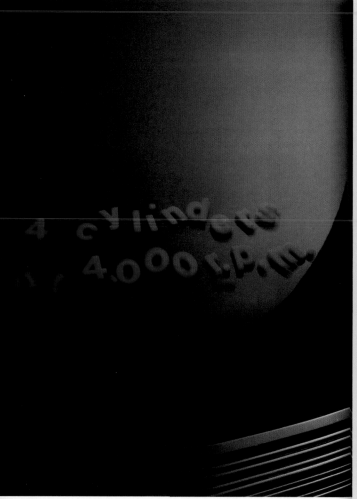

ILLUSTRATION 110

Vogue, 1988

Audi also initiated a hugely successful advertising campaign in the 1980s. The *Vorsprung durch technik* (progress through technology) campaign started in 1984 and played on the German stereotype of meticulous and pedantic engineers and technicians. A clever advertisement by Citroën from 1989 **ILLUSTRATION 111** spoofs the well-known car advertising slogans of the time, including the Audi one. In the advertisement, the Peugeot lion is replaced with a tortoise and the BMW's 'ultimate' machine is turned into an 'intimate' one! This deliberately self-deprecating advertisement by Citroën for the 2CV cleverly celebrates the low-tech and low-priced reputation of a car which had been a best-seller since 1948. It was originally designed for French farmers for off-road driving and famously could carry a basket of eggs across a ploughed field without breaking them! The car was so popular when it was launched that second-hand models were more expensive than new ones, because they would allow buyers to avoid the long waiting list.

Another memorable car advertising campaign of the 1980s was for Volvo. Safety was becoming a major theme of the period. In Britain in January 1983, legislation came into force making it compulsory for drivers and front seat passengers to wear seat belts. It is estimated that by 2003, over 50,000 lives had been saved by the new regulation. Volvo had been the first car to offer safety belts as standard and, since then, safety, reliability and durability have been recurrent themes in Volvo advertising. An advertisement for the 740 Turbo in 1987 used a clever image of someone trying to pull a resistant crash test dummy out of the car. This image not only emphasised the association of the brand with thorough safety testing, but also implied that even the inanimate dummy could be seduced by the pleasure of driving the vehicle **ILLUSTRATION 112.**

ILLUSTRATION 111

1989

Reproduced courtesy of Citroën UK Ltd

WHAT THE 2CV NEEDS IS A SNAPPY SLOGAN.

THE INTIMATE DRIVING MACHINE!
There's nothing like a 2CV for bringing the family closer.

FRONTIERS WITHOUT TECHNOLOGY!
Even without a turbocharger, cruise control or on-board computer, we somehow get along.

FOUR SPRUNG SEATS FOR PICNIC!
At last the answer to back-seat drivers: a removable rear seat.

THE TORTOISE GOES FROM STRENGTH TO STRENGTH!
Or even, on a good day, from 0 to 71.5 mph.

ONCE BITTEN, FOREVER CITROËN!
At £3,980 on the road, what 2CV driver could ever afford to change?

CITROËN 2CV

ONE TEST DRIVE AND YOU'RE HOOKED.

Power. Acceleration. Excitement.

Can this be a Volvo of which we speak? Indeed it can.

Besides providing the expected safety, reliability and dependability, the Volvo 740 Turbo is unexpectedly powerful. A turbo-charged 2.3 litre fuel-injected engine will pull you

from 0 to 60 mph in 7.7 seconds (182 bhp puts the Porsche 944 to shame) and can notch up a top speed of 124 mph.

Delivery of power, especially between 30 and 50 mph, is remarkably smooth and swift.

And the 740 Turbo's overdrive enables a cruising

speed of 70 mph at well below 3,000 rpm. Bliss.

Alloy wheels, low-profile tyres, power steering and a leather/plush interior make it even harder to tear yourself away.

So be on the safe side when you take a test drive.

Take a cheque book.

To: Volvo, Springfield House, Princess Street, Bristol BS3 4EF. For a brochure, call 0800 400 430 free, or post the coupon.
Mr/Mrs/Miss ___
Address ___
___ Postcode ___ Tel: ___

VOLVO 740 TURBO SALOON. £16,610.

THE VOLVO 740 AND 760 SALOONS. PRICES FROM £11,910 TO £20,490 INCLUDING CAR TAX AND VAT (EXCL. STANDARD NATIONAL DELIVERY CHARGE £165, INC. VAT). PRICES CORRECT AT TIME OF GOING TO PRESS. FOR CUSTOMER INFORMATION TELEPHONE, IPSWICH (0473) 270270.

ILLUSTRATION 112

The Sunday Times Magazine, 1987

ILLUSTRATION 113

1985

IF IT CAN START IN HERE, IT CAN START IN GUILDFORD.

VOLVO 340DL £4995

In an advertisement for Volvo dated 1985, the viewer is asked to think about Volvo's reputation for reliability and the advantage of having a car that will start in all weather conditions. The image shows a car encased in ice and we are informed by the copy that it had been left in a cold store for over a day, after which the engine was then started at the first attempt. This message is not immediately apparent solely from the image or the tag-line, and the viewer is challenged to work it out for him/herself, or to spend time reading the small print **ILLUSTRATION 113**.

ILLUSTRATION 114

The Sunday Times Magazine, 1987

Saab is a Swedish car company often in direct competition with its rival Volvo. The company was formed in 1937 and originally manufactured aeroplanes. In a 1987 advertisement, Saab used its reputation in aircraft development to distinguish itself from other car companies, particularly its main rival, by declaring that its own safety policy was modelled on planes rather than tanks. The text is alluding to a comparison that was often made between Volvo cars and those inelegant military vehicles. The image makes a point about style, even though most of the car is not visible, but the copy emphasises safety **ILLUSTRATION 114**.

"Before I'll ride with a drunk, I'll drive myself." —*Stevie Wonder*

Driving after drinking, or riding with a driver who's been drinking, is a big mistake. Anyone can see that.

This poster of Stevie Wonder should help stop teenagers from killing themselves. Reader's Digest is putting it in more than 16,000 schools across America—as part of our challenge to students to devise programs against drinking and driving. This June the Reader's Digest Foundation will award $500,000 in four year scholarships to the students who devised the best programs. To learn more contact your high school principal.

ILLUSTRATION 115

Reader's Digest, 1986

As part of the safety themes of the era, there were numerous campaigns in Britain and America during the 1980s against drink-driving. Drink-driving laws were enhanced during this time in the United States, mainly due to pressure from groups like Mothers Against Drink Driving (MADD) and perhaps as a result of clever adverts like this one published in *Reader's Digest* in 1986 **ILLUSTRATION 115**. In Britain, equivalent advertising campaigns were run and during the 1980s the number of casualties as a result of drink-driving reduced considerably.

So in an age where car advertising focused on safety, rationalism and practicality while also developing the art of persuasive photography, it can also be seen that the emphasis seemed to be on exclusive and expensive cars, particularly those that linked themselves with images of success and power. This was the period of economic polarisation in both Britain and America when many experienced a decline in their living standards, while some made huge profits from rising company and property values. Car advertising was primarily directed at the beneficiaries of this new wealth. An advertisement for Rover in 1981 epitomises the style and intention of this kind of campaign to appeal to the new breed of the 'upwardly mobile' and wealthy **ILLUSTRATION 116**. The car is photographed in such a way to emphasise power and superiority, and the text, 'formula for success', along with the familiar Rover tag-line 'success breeds success', attempts to attract those who had made their fortunes in the 1980s boom.

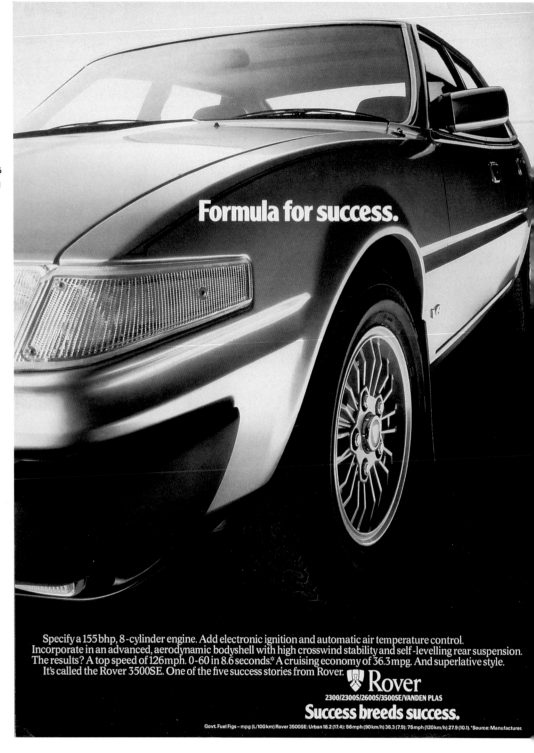

Formula for success.

Specify a 155 bhp, 8-cylinder engine. Add electronic ignition and automatic air temperature control. Incorporate in an advanced, aerodynamic bodyshell with high crosswind stability and self-levelling rear suspension. The results? A top speed of 126 mph. 0-60 in 8.6 seconds.* A cruising economy of 36.3 mpg. And superlative style. It's called the Rover 3500SE. One of the five success stories from Rover.

Rover

2300/2300S/2600S/3500SE/VANDEN PLAS

Success breeds success.

Govt. Fuel Figs – mpg (L/100 km) Rover 3500SE: Urban 16.2 (17.4): 56 mph (90 km/h) 36.3 (7.9): 75 mph (120 km/h) 27.9 (10.1).*Source: Manufacturer.

Chapter 9

1990s

Think big

n the 1990s, car advertisers seemed to develop a new sophistication and a respect for their audiences. Perhaps these advertisers were influenced by the hugely successful surreal and humorous tobacco campaigns which had developed as a response to advertising restrictions. Advertising campaigns such as those for Silk Cut by Saatchi & Saatchi, and for Benson & Hedges by the Collett Dickenson Pearce agency, ushered in a new era of advertising techniques using high-quality photographic images that challenged the viewer to interpret visual clues. These work on the theory that the more you are forced to use your imagination, the more you will remember. An advertisement for Volkswagen from 1994 makes an unsubtle reference to tobacco advertising techniques **ILLUSTRATION 117**. The message is not immediately clear, but after examining the image and text, the viewer understands that the Volkswagen Umwalt diesel is designed to produce cleaner emissions. The text 'extra mild' is a clear reference to cigarettes and supposedly healthier fumes.

Car advertising in the 1990s seemed to focus more on the promotion of brands rather than particular models. This may have been because individual model designs were generally less distinctive than they had been in past decades and companies were learning that brand recognition and trust were more effective techniques towards the end of the century. Mercedes-Benz associated itself with the enduring power of Marilyn Monroe to attract attention long after her death, by

New Volkswagen Extra Mild.

ILLUSTRATION 117

1994

ILLUSTRATION 118

1997

transforming her famous facial beauty-mark into its corporate symbol **ILLUSTRATION 118**. This advertisement is not promoting any particular model, but the general brand image. Honda also put emphasis on the image of its brand rather than the car itself. Honda's advertisement from 1996, published in American magazines, presents the viewer with an impressive selection of hair-style options. The advertisement attracts us, not only by using humorous detail, but also by suggesting a simple and logical solution to perennial problems created by choice and decision-making **ILLUSTRATION 119**.

ILLUSTRATION 119

Rolling Stone, 1996

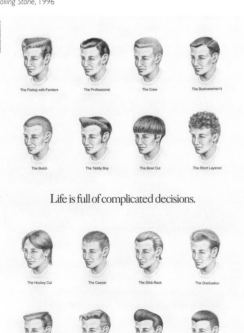

Life is full of complicated decisions.

Simplify.

Sporty. Responsive. And, you won't be embarrassed to be seen with one. What decision could be easier? **HONDA**
The Accord Coupe.

{$} *Perception*

{ $ } *Reality*

More room. More refined. More fun. The new Civic Coupe. HONDA

..., 1-800-33-HONDA, ext.389. Internet: http://www.honda.com
...an Honda Motor Co., Inc.

ILLUSTRATION 120
Rolling Stone, 1995

Through the 1990s BMW continued its series of imaginative and innovative advertising campaigns. In the 1980s the company started to run a series of April Fools' Day advertisements which have continued right up to today. The advertisements feature made-up 'innovations' and 'features' such as a steering wheel which changes side for continental driving and a convertible that can keep out the rain when the roof is open! One of the best was for the 'IDS', an 'Insect Deflector Screen' which would allow insects to bounce off the windscreen rather than splatter untidily on the glass.

The economic realities of recession in the 1990s meant that customers were especially conscious of value for money. Many of those that made large fortunes in the 1980s had to be more careful about their spending. Car advertising often emphasised the value of the product while reassuring customers that it would still look like the car belonging to a wealthy and successful person. An American advertisement for the Honda Civic coupe, dated 1995, conveys this simple message using direct and unambiguous words and symbols **ILLUSTRATION 120**. An advertisement for Ford's embarrassingly unsubtly named

DRIVE A BARGAIN, HARD.

FORD PROBE SE

Ford Probe SE is one car with looks that deliver. Its sleek, aerodynamic body and road-hugging profile are your first clues that this car can really handle. Balanced on a special handling suspension

with a low, wide stance, this is a car that was meant to be driven... and driven hard.

Option package savings make it very affordable to drive a Probe SE, well equipped with:

• 2.0 liter DOHC 16-valve engine
• 4-wheel independent suspension
• Air conditioning
• Electronic AM/FM stereo cassette
• 15" aluminum wheels
• Standard dual air bags* and more.

Great features at a great price make Ford Probe SE a true bargain. Great performance makes it the kind of bargain you'll want to drive hard.

*Always wear your safety belt.

HAVE YOU DRIVEN A FORD LATELY?

Ford

ILLUSTRATION 121

Rolling Stone, 1995

'Probe' model in 1995 not only suggests good value, but has macho-sexual connotations **ILLUSTRATION 121**. Ford introduced Probe in 1989 to replace the Ford EXP as the company's sport compact car, but sales were disappointing and the model was finally discontinued in 1997.

A very clever and memorable campaign for Volkswagen Polo in the late 1990s created scenarios based on the idea that viewers would be so distracted and surprised by the reasonable price of the car, that accidents and

mishaps would result. In one of the advertisements, a wedding photo was ruined because the photographer was focusing on the low price of the Volkswagen advertisement in the background **ILLUSTRATION 122**. Other advertisements in the same series featured distracted pedestrians colliding with street-lamps. Volkswagen continued its talent for using innovative, successful, humorous and challenging advertising with an award-winning advertisement for the Sharan which featured a simple image of a shark with a drawn-on mouth and pipe. The text reads 'Power in Disguise', a

The Sharan. Power in disguise.
174 bhp in a MPV body. For a brochure call 0800 333 666.

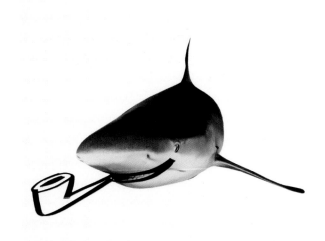

ILLUSTRATION 122
1999

ILLUSTRATION 123
2000

clever and amusing use of visuals to define the message **ILLUSTRATION 123**. The advertising campaign that was so famously initiated by Bill Bernbach in the 1960s for the VW Beetle continues to this day. The advertisements have become immediately recognisable and have defined the product over the years. A Beetle advertisement from

1999 not only makes visual reference to the famous 'Think Small' image of 1961 by using a small photograph of the car and bravely retaining lots of white space on the page, but also refers to the iconic model's traditional, unusual and unchanging style by using the text 'Other cars are starting to look funny' **ILLUSTRATION 124**.

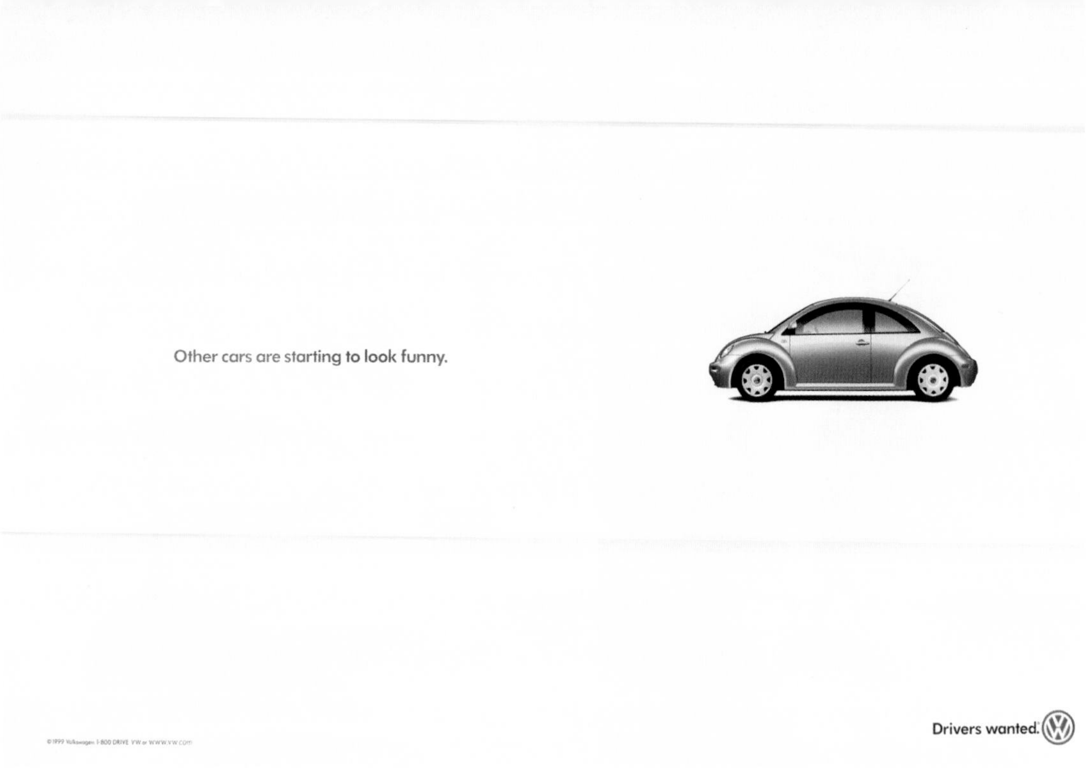

Other cars are starting **to look funny.**

©1999 Volkswagen 1 800 DRIVE VW or www.vw.com

Drivers wanted. Ⓥ

ILLUSTRATION 124

GQ, 1999

Concern for the environment and the effects of car emissions on global warming started to re-emerge as an issue, having been largely ignored by manufacturers and customers in the 1980s. Concerns about car emissions in the 1970s had been partly addressed with computer engine management systems which improved efficiency and reduced emissions. In the 1980s, more efficient engines led to an increase in the production of more powerful cars. By the 1990s, an average passenger car would often have been as powerful (about 200 horsepower) as a sports car in the 1980s. Catalytic converters, devices that reduce the toxicity of engine emissions, became popular and Volkswagen developed a memorable advertising image in 1992 to market its catalytic Polo **ILLUSTRATION 125**. The cartoon depiction by Mel Calman, a cartoonist for *The Times,* shows his trademark 'little man' driving a car which is emitting a cloud of clean, blue air in the midst of a dirty, dark fug.

Unfortunately, despite the new awareness of environmental damage, the fashion for larger and more powerful cars continued to grow. The success of the Renault Espace was an early sign of what the large family car would become. It was the first multi-purpose vehicle (mpv) with space for seven passengers that didn't look like a commercial van. After a slow start (a month after its launch in 1984, only nine had been sold), the Espace went on to become extremely popular and demand continued to exceed supply for all models right up to the Espace IV which was launched in 2003. A 1999 advertisement shows that the company had learned that customers were willing to pay for the feeling of space, height and luxury that this mpv could provide **ILLUSTRATION 126**. The advertisement cleverly merges the image of an exotic swimming pool with the ocean to create the illusion of a huge man-made pool, although it takes the viewer several 'looks' to work out the message of the Magritte-like illusion. As drivers'

ILLUSTRATION 125
1992

From the front, few small cars are as attractive as our new Polo.

From the back, though, we're tempted to say no small car is as attractive as our new Polo.

Because no other small cars come with a catalytic converter as standard. An advanced 'three-way' catalyst at that.

One capable of reducing by more than 90% the trio of toxic pollutants in exhaust fumes.

It may not be perfect but it's 90% more perfect than no 'cat' at all.

That said, you may be wondering what sort of effect this has on the Polo's performance.

Wonder not. Thanks to the introduction of fuel injection, it's well up to speed.

The brakes are now servo. So stopping suddenly gives you even less of a start.

And not least, the uprated suspension makes for even nimbler handling and an even smoother ride.

All in all, you could say our new Polo leaves the competition behind.

But very little else.

The new catalytic Polo.

ILLUSTRATION 126
Vogue, 1999

Isn't space the ultimate luxury?

Room to think. Room to breathe. Room to manoeuvre. Room to be yourself. Room for nothing to be left behind. That's what the new Espace gives you. With foldable, reversible, removable and continuously adjustable seating, remote-control Hi-Fi, air-conditioning and a choice of engines (3 litre 24-valve V6, 2 litre 16-valve or turbo-diesel) the new Espace is the ultimate luxury. Prices from £19,200.

For more information, call 0800 52 51 50 or visit www.renault.co.uk

Espace

RENAULT

ILLUSTRATION 127

Vogue, 1999

experiences of traffic congestion, road works, diversions and road rage increased, so grew the desire for a feeling of space, elevation and distance in the protective bubble of an automobile interior.

The huge growth in popularity of the sport utility vehicle (SUV) in the early 1990s, first in America and then in Britain, was partly due to the low oil prices of the period. Prior to this rise in popularity, SUVs were usually bought only by rural drivers for use in off-road situations. SUVs then became attractive to urban drivers because of the large interiors, higher ride and perceived safety for them and their families. Advertising for these kinds of vehicles

originally emphasised practicality and safety, but they eventually crossed over into the high-powered luxury car market. Astonishingly, SUVs now command more than half the world's automobile market. An advertisement for the Jeep Cherokee from 1999 is a vibrant mélange of images evoking the adventure of driving in the wilds of the American plains **ILLUSTRATION 127**. Nevertheless, the advertisers knew that the majority of buyers for this kind of vehicle would not be driving the car off-road: the text 'Adrenalin rush hour' suggests to the viewer that they will feel the excitement of the power and acceleration of the car even if they are only likely to be encountering the everyday challenges of urban streets.

The Ka Black. A limited edition of 1000. Available with black metallic paint, black bumpers, air-conditioned black leather interior, black leather steering wheel, black leather gear knob, black carpets and of course black tyres. Just as Henry would have wanted it.

the ford**ka** black · *Ford*

ILLUSTRATION 128

Vogue, 1999

An advertisement for the Ford Ka Black in 1999 is an example of how messages and slogans come full circle **ILLUSTRATION 128**. The famous saying attributed to Henry Ford and quoted in his own autobiography, 'Any customer can have a car painted any color that he wants so long as it is black', is revived to advertise the all-black Ka model. The text declares that its colour is 'just as Henry would have wanted it', but it is unlikely that Henry Ford would have approved of the emphasis of style over practicality and cost.

Expenditure on automobile advertising shows no sign of slowing down. In the year 2000, six billion euros were spent on car advertising in Europe and in America in 2003, over ten billion dollars were spent. So, even with the environmental concerns that dominate this era, car companies and their advertisers are developing ever-more innovative ways of persuading us to spend increasingly large proportions of our income on what have become symbols of our status and aspirations. As the century ended with customers choosing cars of a style that brings to mind the strange construction of vehicles one hundred years before, the persuasive power of car advertising ensures that the familiar slogans, brands, logos and advertising styles of the major car manufacturers have become universally recognisable.

ALVIS CAR & ENGINEERING COMPANY LTD – a company established in Coventry in 1919. Rover took a controlling interest in Alvis in 1965 and Alvis cars continued to be produced until 1967. The name is now owned by BAE Systems.

AUSTIN MOTOR COMPANY – formed by Herbert Austin in 1905 at Longbridge, later part of Birmingham. Its most famous product was the Austin Seven (or Austin Se7en), to become known as the 'Mini'. The company merged with the Nuffield Organisation in 1952 to become the British Motor Corporation which then became part of the British Leyland Motor Corporation in 1968.

BENTLEY – a British manufacturer of luxury cars founded by Walter Owen Bentley in 1919. The company was taken over by the Volkswagen Group in 1998.

BMW – Bayerische Motoren Werke (Bavarian Motor Works) is a German automobile manufacturer founded by Franz Josef Popp, Max Friz, and Camillo Castiglioni in 1916 (at which time it was known as Bayerische Flugzeugwerke or BFW). BMW currently owns the Rolls-Royce and Mini brands.

BRITISH LEYLAND – the British Leyland Motor Corporation Ltd formed in 1968, was partly nationalised in 1975, becoming known as British Leyland. It was renamed as the Rover Group in 1986 but went bankrupt in 2005 marking the end of mass car production by British owned manufacturers.

BRITISH MOTOR CORPORATION – (BMC) a car manufacturing company that was formed in 1952 when the Nuffield Organisation merged with Austin. In 1968 it became part of the British Leyland Motor Corporation.

BSA – (Birmingham Small Arms Company) was the largest motorcycle producer in the world during the 1950s. The company purchased Daimler in 1910 and Lanchester in 1931.

BUICK – the Buick Motor Company was established in 1903 by David Dunbar Buick in Detroit, Michigan. It became the largest car maker in America under its new manager William C Durant who took over the company in 1904. Durant had founded General Motors of which Buick remains a major division.

CADILLAC – a brand of luxury vehicles owned by General Motors. The firm was formed in 1902 and was named after a French explorer, Antoine de La Mothe Cadillac, who founded Detroit in 1701.

CHEVROLET – a brand owned by General Motors and co-founded in 1911 by Louis Chevrolet and William C Durant who was also the founder of General Motors.

CHRYSLER – founded in 1925 by Walter P Chrysler and now the largest private car maker in North America. Mainly owned by Cerberus Capital Management from 2007 and now known as Chrysler LLC.

CITROËN – founded by André Citroën in France in 1919. His factory had built armaments during the First World War and switched to cars when the war ended. Since 1976 the company has been part of PSA Peugeot Citroën.

DAIMLER – the Daimler Motor Company was founded in 1896 by Frederick Simms who had bought the UK patent rights to the German engineer Gottlieb Daimler's engine, designed specifically for motor vehicles. This company is not to be confused with Daimler-Benz AG, a

German engine and car manufacturer established in 1926 which produced the Mercedes-Benz brand.

DATSUN – a Japanese brand name used by DAT Motors and Nissan. The brand was discontinued in 1986.

DETROIT ELECTRIC – a brand produced by Anderson Electric Car Company in Detroit. Produced from 1907 to 1939.

DUNLOP – a tyre company established in 1889 in Dublin by John Boyd Dunlop, a Scottish vet.

FIAT – an Italian car company based in Turin and founded in 1899 by Giovanni Agnelli. FIAT stands for Fabbrica Italiana Automobili Torino (Italian Automobile Factory of Turin).

FISHER – an automobile coachbuilder founded by the Fisher brothers in 1908 in Detroit which is now an operating division of General Motors. Fisher Body's started as a horse-drawn carriage shop in Norwalk, Ohio in the late 1800s.

FORD – the Ford Motor Company is the world's third largest car manufacturer after General Motors and Toyota. It was founded by Henry Ford in 1903 and has been run by members of the Ford family ever since.

FRANKLIN – the H.H. Franklin Manufacturing Company made air-cooled cars from 1902 to 1934 in Syracuse, New York.

GENERAL MOTORS – GM was the world's largest car manufacturer during the twentieth century. Founded in 1908 by William C Durant who had previously manufactured horse-drawn carriages. The company was initially a holding company for Buick Motor Company and went on to buy Oldsmobile, Cadillac, Pontiac and many others. Chevrolet, Vauxhall, Saab, Daewoo and Opel all became part of the growing company.

HILLMAN – a British company founded by William Hillman and Louis Coatalen in 1907. It was taken over by Rootes in 1931 and was later acquired by Chrysler until control was passed to Peugeot in 1979.

HONDA – a Japanese company formally established by Siochiro Honda in 1948 after the Second World War. It began as a manufacturer of scooters and motorcycles. Siochiro Honda ran the company until 1973.

HUMBER – a British car once favoured by royalty and the ruling classes. Established as a bicycle manufacturing company in 1868 by Thomas Humber. It became part of the Rootes Group in 1931.

HUPMOBILE – a car produced by the Hupp Motor Company of Detroit, Michigan. The company was founded by brothers Robert and Louis Hupp in 1908. Hupmobiles had the reputation for being dependable and economical and were used by the American army in the First World War as ambulances.

JAGUAR – a car produced by Jaguar Cars Ltd which was a company established by William Lyons and William Walmsley as the Swallow Sidecar Company in Blackpool in 1922. Moving to Whitley, Coventry in 1934, the company became part of British Leyland in 1968. It was under Ford ownership in the 1990s and 2000s. The company was sold by Ford to the Indian company Tata in 2008.

JEEP – see Willys-Overland

JORDAN MOTOR CAR COMPANY – a car manufacturing company established by Edward S 'Ned' Jordan in 1916 in Cleveland Ohio. Perhaps more famous for its innovative advertising than the cars themselves, the company ceased production in 1931.

LANCHESTER – the Lanchester Motor Company was established in 1895 by brothers Frederick, George and Frank Lanchester. The company merged with Daimler in 1931 which was then owned by BSA and later by Ford. The Lanchester name was phased out after 1955.

LAND-ROVER – a four-wheel drive utility vehicle designed by Maurice Wilks of Rover which was first shown in 1948. Wilks used plentiful aircraft aluminium, which was resistant to corrosion, as steel was in such short supply in the post-war period. The brand was later produced by different owners including British Leyland, British Aerospace and BMW. It was sold to Ford in 2000 and then on to Indian company Tata in 2008.

LIBERTY MOTOR CAR COMPANY – a company established by Percy Owens in Detroit in 1916. Only one model was produced, the Liberty Six. Because of financial difficulties the company went into receivership in 1923.

LINCOLN – the Lincoln Motor Company was founded by Henry M Leland in 1917 to build aircraft engines for World War I. The company went through a difficult conversion to being a luxury car manufacturer after the war and was finally bought out by Henry Ford in 1922. Lincoln provides official state limousines for American Presidents; indeed, John Kennedy was assassinated in a 1961 Lincoln Continental convertible.

MARMON MOTOR CARS – the Marmon Wasp was a racing car that won the first Indianapolis 500 race in 1911. Howard Marmon's company went on to produce luxury automobiles but the factory closed in 1932 as a result of the Great Depression.

MAXWELL CARS – originally the Maxwell-Briscoe Company of Tarrytown, New York and established in 1904. The company failed and assets were absorbed by Chrysler in 1925.

MERCEDES-BENZ – a German brand of luxury vehicles. The company dates from the 'Agreement of Mutual Interest' signed in 1924 by the Benz company and Daimler-Motoren-Gesellschaft. Gottlieb Daimler named his cars after his daughter Mercedes after he had sold the rights to his name to a British company.

MG – a British sports car brand originally created by the Morris Garages Company from 1924. The company was an offshoot of the larger Morris Motors. The company became half of MG Rover in 2000 and then was bought by the Chinese company Nanjing Automobile Group in 2005.

MINI – the all-time best-selling British car. Designed by Alec Issigonis and launched by the British Motor Corporation in 1959. The first models were marketed as the Austin Se7en and the Morris Mini-Minor. (Austin and Morris were both BMC brands). The cost of the 1959 model was £496.

MORRIS MOTOR COMPANY – established by William Morris (later Viscount Nuffield), a bicycle manufacturer in 1910 in Cowley, Oxford. In 1924 Morris overtook Ford to become Britain's biggest car manufacturer. Morris became part of the Nuffield Organisation in 1938. The brand name was used until the early 1980s when the Cowley plant was converted to produce Austin and Rover cars.

NUFFIELD ORGANISATION – a British car manufacturing company formed in 1938 by William Morris, Viscount Nuffield, as a merger of Morris Motor Company, MG and Riley. The company merged with the Austin Motor Company to form the British Motor Corporation in 1952.

OLDS MOTOR VEHICLE COMPANY – established in 1897 by Ransom Eli Olds in Lansing, Michigan. Olds produced the first mass produced car, the Oldsmobile Curved Dash Runabout in 1901.

PACKARD – a luxury American automobile first produced by brothers James Ward and William Doud Packard in 1899 in Warren, Ohio. Famous for the advertising line, 'ask the man who owns one'. The Packard Motor Car Company bought Studebaker in 1954 creating the Studebaker-Packard Corporation. The brand ended in 1958.

PEUGEOT – a French vehicle producing company established by the Peugeot family which had been involved in steel production since 1810. The company produced the first Peugeot car in 1889. Peugeot took over the Citroën car manufacturing company in 1975 to form the PSA (Peugeot Société Anonyme) group.

PLYMOUTH – a low-priced marque first introduced by the Chrysler Corporation in 1928. It was produced until 2001. Labelled as one of 'the low-priced three' along with Chevrolet and Ford.

PONTIAC – a medium-priced marque produced by General Motors from 1926.

PORSCHE – a German car manufacturer specialising in prestigious sports cars. Founded in 1931 by Ferdinand Porsche.

RENAULT – a hugely successful French vehicle manufacturer founded in 1899 as the Société Renault Frères by brothers Louis, Marcel and Fernand Renault. Louis Renault died in prison in 1944 after having been accused of collaboration during the Nazi occupation of France.

RILEY – a British car and bicycle manufacturer from 1890. The company became part of the Nuffield Organisation in 1938. The production of Riley cars ended in 1969.

ROLLS-ROYCE – established in 1906 by Frederick Henry Royce and Charles Stewart Rolls. In the original agreement, Royce manufactured the cars and Rolls sold them. The company soon developed a reputation for producing cars of the highest standards of quality and luxury. Rolls-Royce cars have been produced by BMW since 1998.

ROOTES GROUP – a British car manufacturing company originally founded in Kent by William Rootes in 1919. The company became known for building dependable mid-range cars. Rootes was parent company of Hillman, Humber, Singer, Sunbeam and Talbot cars. It was taken over by Chrysler in the 1960s.

ROVER – originally a bicycle manufacturer in Coventry, Rover became a successful British motor vehicle company moving to Solihull after World War II. The company became part of Leyland Motors in 1967 and then as the Rover Group was successively owned by British Aerospace, BMW and Ford. Sold to Indian company Tata Motors in 2008.

SAAB – a company established in 1938 to supply aircraft to the Royal Swedish Air Force in preparation for World War II. Needing to diversify after the end of the war, the first prototype automobile, the Ursaab, was produced in 1947. SAAB is an acronym for Svenska Aeroplan Aktiebolaget (Swedish Aeroplane Corporation)

SPORT UTILITY VEHICLE – a passenger vehicle with the towing capability equivalent to a pick-up truck for off and on-road driving. Also known as 'off-road vehicle', 'four-wheel-drive' or just '4WD' or '4X4'.

STUDEBAKER – an American car manufacturer based in Indiana. Founded in 1852 as a producer of mining wagons, the company started building electric cars in 1902, moving on to petrol cars in 1904. Studebaker stopped building cars in 1966.

TOYOTA – a multinational company based in Japan. The company built its first passenger car in 1936. Toyota, along with GM Motors competes to be the world's largest car manufacturer. Its brands include Scion and Lexus and, in part, Daihatsu, Subaru and Isuzu.

TRIUMPH – a British car company which originated as the Triumph Cycle Company in 1897. It changed its name to the Triumph Motor Company in 1930. After hitting hard times, the company was liquidated and the brand name was bought by Standard Motor Company in 1944. Bought by Leyland Motors in 1960, the last Triumph model, the Acclaim, was launched in 1981. The brand name is now owned by BMW.

VAUXHALL – a company founded by Alexander Wilson in 1857 building pumps and marine engines in Vauxhall, London. The company was bought by General Motors in 1925. Today, most Vauxhall models are right-hand-drive versions of GM's Opel cars.

VOLKSWAGEN – one of the world's largest car producers based in Wolfsburg, Germany. In 1934, Dr Ferdinand Porsche agreed to design the 'people's car' for Adolf Hitler, chancellor of Germany. A factory was built in 1938 and some prototypes were made before the war, but production didn't take off until around 1948 when Major Ivan Hirst of the British Military Government instigated mass-production.

VOLKSWAGEN BEETLE – a distinctive small car originally produced in Germany from the late 1940s. Sales soared in the early 1960s in America and in 1972 the Beetle overtook the Ford Model T as the most produced single model car with over fifteen million made. Production of the Beetle stopped in 2003.

VOLKSWAGEN GOLF – a small family, front-wheel-drive car launched in Europe in 1974. Debuted as the 'Rabbit' in America in 1975. Designed by Giorgetto Giugiaro and his Italdesign studio. The Golf GTI, with a 110 horse-power engine, was launched in 1976.

VOLVO – a Swedish company founded in 1927 with a reputation for building safe cars. The name is derived from the Latin for 'I roll'. Owned by AB Volvo until 1999 when it was bought by Ford.

WILLYS-OVERLAND – in 1908, John North Willys bought the Overland Automotive Division of the Standard Wheel Company and created the Willys-Overland Motor Company. The company is best known for producing the Jeep, a general purpose vehicle for military and civilian use. The name Jeep is thought to have originated from the shortening of the abbreviation GP for 'general purpose'.

WOLSELEY – the origin of this famous British car make is in the Wolseley Sheep Shearing Company which was established by the engineer Frederick Wolseley. Wolseley's first car was designed in 1895 by Herbert Austin who went on to establish the Austin Motor Company in 1905. The first Wolseley car to be sold to the public was in 1901. The Wolseley company was purchased by Lord Nuffield in 1926. The name was used until 1975. The Wolseley marque was transferred to Nanjing Automobile Group as part of MG Rover's assets in 2005.

WOLSELEY-SIDDELEY – the Wolseley company purchased the Siddeley Autocar Company in 1905 and the marque was renamed Wolseley-Siddeley until 1910.

BIBLIOGRAPHY

GARTMAN, David (1994) *Auto Opium: a Social History of American Automobile Design*, Routledge, London and New York

GLANCEY, Jonathan (2003) *The Car: A History of the Automobile*, Carlton Books, London

IKUTA, Yasutoshi (1988a) *The American Automobile: Advertising from the Antique and Classic Eras*, Chronicle Books, San Francisco

IKUTA, Yasutoshi (1988b) *Cruise O Matic, Automobile Advertising of the 1950s*, Chronicle Books, San Francisco

MCLUHAN, Marshall (1964) *Understanding Media*, Routledge & Kegan Paul

O'CONNELL, Sean (1998) *The Car in British Society: Class, Gender and Motoring 1896-1939*, Manchester University Press

ROBERTS, Peter (1976) *Any Color so Long as it's Black: The First Fifty Years of Automobile Advertising*, David & Charles, Canada

ROSPA, Royal Society for the Prevention of Accidents, www.rospa.com

SAUNDERS, Dave (1999) *20th Century Advertising*, Carlton, London

STEVENSON, Heon (1995) *Selling the Dream: Advertising the American Automobile 1930-1980*, Academy, London

STEVENSON, Heon (2005) *British Car Advertising of the 1960s*, McFarland & Co Inc, London

STEWART, Catherine (1995) *Superbrands: An Insight into 50 of the World's Superbrands*, Special Event Books, Horsham

WALKER LAIRD, Pamela (1996) 'The car without a single weakness': early automobile advertising, *Technology and Culture*, volume 37, part 4

WILLSON, Quentin (2001) *Cars: A Celebration*, Dorling Kindersley, London

WOLLEN, Peter and KERR, Joe (2002) *Autopia: Cars and Culture*, Reaktion Books, London

ZUNBRUNN, Michel (2004) Text by Robert Cunberford, *Auto Legends: Classics of Style and Design*, Merrell, London